Near to the Brokenhearted

Funeral Sermon Outlines

EDITED BY

Rickey Collum

AND

John Young

CYPRESS

Published by Cypress Publications

Copyright © 2024 edited by Rickey Collum and John Young

Manufactured in the United States of America

Cataloging-in-Publication Data

Near to the brokenhearted: funeral sermon outlines/edited by Rickey Collum and John Young

p. cm.

ISBN 978-1-956811-91-9 (pbk.); 978-1-956811-92-6 (ebook)

1. Funeral sermons—Outlines, syllabi, etc. I. Collum, Rickey, editor. II. Young, John, editor. III. Title.

251.02—dc20

Cover design by Brad McKinnon and Brittany Vander Maas.

For information:

Cypress Publications
3625 Helton Drive,
PO Box HCU,
Florence, AL 35630

www.hcu.edu

CONTENTS

INTRODUCTION
RICKEY COLLUM

How can anyone put into words or introduce someone that changed their life forever? This is my battle as I try to share with you my mentor, advocate, and friend, Jack P. Wilhelm. I could tell you how he was always in my corner. How he was there when I needed him, time and time again. But what I most want you to see is that it was not just me, but thousands of Church of Christ preachers throughout the brotherhood who benefited from Jack's willingness to share his knowledge and wisdom with others. It has been estimated that as many as 1,000 congregations might have heard sermons that ministers adapted from his published materials.

From 1980 until 1992, Jack Wilhelm, through his publishing company Cox Creek Bookstore, distributed a free newsletter called R.S.V.P. These four letters of the alphabet were not random but stood for Relevant, Scriptural, Varied, Practical sermon outlines. However, at one time, I believe I also heard a story that those same letters stood for Roots, Stem, Vines, and Petals. This probably goes back to Jesus's statement in John 15:5. R.S.V.P. was sent out monthly and usually contained four sermons and a few comical items used for filler, which often ended up in church bulletins around the country.

The work that went into the R.S.V.P. was very time-consuming and accomplished while Jack was preaching full-time and was President of Mars Hill Bible School in Florence Alabama. So not only was he helping preachers who were sick or unable to prepare a lesson, with good sound sermon outlines, he was helping mold young minds and preaching himself. There are so many testimonials and stories about how the R.S.V.P. newsletter helped someone or encouraged preachers.

My favorite was one of the few times that Jack and his wife, Mary Alice, (who also served as editor and sounding board of the newsletter), were on a vacation in the mountains. They were looking forward to hearing someone else preach. When arriving at the local church they discovered that 2 visiting students from Freed-Hardeman University would speak, one at the morning service and the other in the evening service. Still, they were looking forward to hearing the young preachers. The student preacher began to preach, and it was not long before Jack and Mary Alice realized the young man was preaching directly from the current R.S.V.P. As they traveled to their hotel, they decided to attend that evening service with the hopes of hearing another lesson from a young preacher. When arriving that evening they heard another preacher preach the exact sermon the earlier preacher had preached from the newsletter.

I have read personally from the many letters sent by preachers with sick children, those battling cancer, some who had been up all night with a sick member of the congregation, the list goes on and on of preachers who used Jack's sermons because they did not have the time or energy to write their own.

In the summer of 2007, a small church asked me to be their preacher. Jack encouraged me to accept the pulpit. He provided me with a stack of his sermons to learn from and to preach. Every week I would put together my own sermon using his Bible verses and sometimes his thoughts and I would email him the sermon and he would correct and polish it and send it back. This went on for the first two years I preached.

When he felt I could write my own sermons, he invited me to Bible Emphasis School for ministers where he taught classes in Athens and Winfield, Alabama. He had been doing this since 1987. I was lucky enough to have 7 years of those long trips in the car with a preacher of 60 years, to pick his brain and learn from his wisdom and the other preachers who attended. During that time, he wrote the *Gospel Advocate's Companion* yearbook for 2003–2004 and 13 *Foundation Quarterlies* for adults from 2004–2007. He wrote additional study books for Lambert Publishing. Jack and Mary Alice have published over 20 books for personal and class studies.

Upon Jack's death on February 7, 2016, I was asked to help with the funeral of my Paul, and I will forever be his Timothy. I have enclosed in this book the words I spoke that day.

The first group of papers Jack delivered to me was a group of 102 funeral sermon outlines. It was a timely delivery because the next week, I had to preach my first funeral to one of my mother's best friends. Jack believed, and we do as well, that too little training is given to preachers about funerals. This is the reason I wanted to include John Young in this book. John is a historian, and while, to my knowledge, John has yet to preach a funeral, I believe his study of the history of preaching would reveal insights helpful to the reader. Funerals have changed throughout history and are different sometimes from city to city.

As a preacher gets older, he begins to preach more funerals. Funerals, unlike sermons, cannot be written in advance. This book should help as a pattern to assist the preacher who might not have preached many funeral sermons or the veteran preacher who might be experiencing a busy week and a funeral was added to the already full schedule.

We may find ourselves having to write funerals for an infant, someone who has lived a very sin-filled life, or someone you have never met. This book was made for these reasons. We hope it is helpful to you in your ministry and brings glory to the kingdom of God.

Funeral Preaching in the Churches of Christ

A Brief Historical Overview

John Young

As someone who has never actually had to deliver a funeral sermon, I may seem like an odd choice to contribute the foreword for a volume like this one, which is entirely dedicated to the rhetorical form. However, I did have the opportunity to contribute an article on the published funeral sermons of the notable Churches of Christ preacher and teacher T.B. Larimore to the *Journal of Christian Studies* in 2024.[1] As is my (unfortunate) habit, I made a mildly self-congratulatory Facebook post to celebrate its publication, and within a few minutes, my now coeditor Rickey Collum had commented that he wanted me to call him about a possible book project. One conversation led to another, and well, here I am.

Although my decade of leading college, young professionals, and educational ministries thankfully did not require me to preach any funeral services, my experience is probably not comparable to that of someone serving in a congregation-wide capacity. After all, we all die, and unless we eschew any kind of commemo-

---

1. John Young, "'…things we deplore may be best for those we love': The Funeral Sermons of T.B. Larimore," *Journal of Christian Studies* 3.3 (September 2024): 83–93.

ration for family and friends, someone is probably going to need to say something, preferably something helpful, for those gathered. The universality of death and the near-universality of the funeral service notwithstanding, preachers within the Churches of Christ have had relatively few tools at their disposal which were crafted specifically for them. To wit: in 2023, homiletics scholar Rob O'Lynn published a rhetorical analysis of funeral preaching from across the broad sweep of the Stone-Campbell, or Restoration, Movement. His aim was to explore the published minister manuals from each stream of the movement, to evaluate their guidance for funeral preaching, and, in turn, to think more carefully about how to incorporate the "Christian hope" into those messages. Yet this proved all but impossible for the Churches of Christ because, quite simply, there wasn't enough written for O'Lynn to compare.[2] And considering society's changing expectations for funerals and the rise in popularity of the "celebration of life" as a supplement to or even replacement for the traditional funeral, as observed by M. Todd Hall in another *Journal of Christian Studies* article,[3] preachers need guidance today as much as they ever have.

And they have long needed it. Combing the shelves at the Heritage Christian University library one afternoon, I—partly purposefully, partly serendipitously, and totally unscientifically—pulled three similar works from the shelves. These included *Sermons for Funeral Occasions*, edited by B.L. Bedwell and published in 1960;[4] *Thoughts for Funeral Sermons*, edited by John D. Cox and published in 1961;[5] and *Rejoice and Weep: Wedding*

---

2. Rob O'Lynn, "The Christian Hope: A Rhetorical Analysis of Funeral Preaching in the Stone-Campbell Movement," *Lexington Theological Quarterly* 53.1–4 (2023): 34–36.
3. M. Todd Hall, "Let's Talk about Funerals," *Journal of Christian Studies* 1.3 (September 2022): 43–54.
4. B.L. Bedwell, ed., *Sermons for Funeral Occasions* (Austin, TX: Firm Foundation Publishing House, 1960).
5. John D. Cox, ed., *Thoughts for Funeral Sermons* (Florence, AL: 1961).

Ceremonies and Funeral Sermons in Memory of E.L. Whitaker, Jr., published by the Memphis School of Preaching Alumni Association in 1998.[6] Like this book, these three all included funeral sermon outlines solicited by the editors and submitted by numerous preachers. Remarkably, given the chronological and geographical proximity of the four collections—John D. Cox and Jack Wilhelm both preached at the Sherrod Avenue Church of Christ here in Florence, Alabama, after all! —there was startlingly little overlap in the names represented. Out of 110 total preachers who had at least one outline included in one of the four volumes, only one minister, Jim Bill McInteer, contributed to more than one collection (Bedwell's and this one).

Yet despite the wide variety of ministers and congregations represented across the four collections, the introductory materials consistently lament the lack of reliable resources for preachers within Churches of Christ. Bedwell claims in his foreword that he has "been unable to find anything like it in print from the pen of gospel preachers. I have looked far and wide for such a book, only to be disappointed."[7] Cox's preface from a year later says that he "has attempted to render a service which he, as a young preacher more than thirty years ago, wished that some older and more experienced gospel preacher would perform."[8] It is my hope that this volume will prove to be a helpful reference on those difficult occasions in which a minister is called to preach a funeral, and that this short foreword will help make it clearer what we already have on the shelf, so to speak, and what we need to do next.

---

6. *Rejoice and Weep: Wedding Ceremonies and Funeral Sermons in Memory of E.L. Whitaker, Jr.,* (Memphis, TN: Memphis School of Preaching Alumni Association, 1998).

7. Bedwell, *Sermons for Funeral Occasions*, unnumbered page.

8. Cox, *Thoughts for Funeral Sermons*, 5.

PROLOGUE

I am grateful for the 17 brethren who submitted to me the following lessons, with permission to share them with others. Many of these brethren are now with us only in memory of themselves. We honor them and appreciate their work of preaching the gospel and advancing the Cause of Christ for many years. I thought you would be interested in some observations about their work at the time they submitted these lessons.—Jack Wilhelm

• **Granville Brown** lived in Murfreesboro, Tennessee, and was always an inspiration to people who saw him preach and teach in spite of physical limitations. A need he suggested was a lesson for a non-Christian.

• **Ralph Burris** lived in Yorktown, Indiana at the time he submitted his lessons. They were in a building program at the time. He is now semi-retired and lives in Jeffersonville, Indiana. His good wife, Geneva, passed away recently. Theirs was the first wedding ceremony I performed.

•**Charles E. Crouch** was leaving Riverwood church to move to Camden, Tennessee when he sent his lessons. I last saw him when I was in a meeting near Jasper, Tennessee where he was living after retiring.

- **Eugene W. Clevenger** was very busy, "getting ready to move to Cleburne, Texas." He was going to work further on his doctorate and had been "taking French and German in addition to preaching and teaching ..." with about "four full-time jobs." He was my Greek teacher when I was a freshman at David Lipscomb College.

- **Wayne Emmons** lived in Barnesville, Georgia when he submitted his lesson. He enclosed also a copy of a monthly publication he was sending out in a mission field. He later pursued a career as an attorney in Memphis, TN. He passed away in September 2010.

- **Joe D. Gray** was working with the Central church in Valdosta, Georgia at the time he sent lessons. He did not add extra personal comments but submitted some extra lessons that filled several needs.

- **Elvis H. Huffard** (1918–2000) at the time lived in Mayfield, Kentucky. He expressed concerns that a poor family might be taken advantage of when planning a funeral and that ministers could be helpful to them.

- **Paul Hunton** preached in Nashville at the time he submitted his lessons. I had an opportunity to see him more often later after he moved to Huntsville, Alabama to work with Madison Academy.

- **A. Harold Kennamer** (1915–2014) at the time was preaching for the University Blvd. church in Denver, Colorado. He lives now in Abilene, Texas. He was born October 8, 1915, and is looking forward to his 96th birthday this year! He baptized my wife, Mary Alice, on July 10, 1949, while in a meeting at New Hope, Alabama.

- **Claud Lamar, Jr.**, a former college classmate, was preaching at Collegeside Church of Christ in Cookeville, Tennessee at the time he sent me his lessons. He mentioned how much an article J. M. Powell had published near that time in the *Gospel Advocate* helped him. His death at an early age was a great loss.

•**Jim Bill McInteer** (1921–2012) was still in his ministry at the West End Church of Christ in Nashville, Tennessee. He sent greetings to me and Mary Alice with best wishes for my new work as we were leaving Nashville to return to Alabama. I began work as president of Mars Hill Bible School and working again at that time with the Eastside church in Sheffield, which is now Cox Boulevard church.

•**John P. Murphree** (1927–2015) preached for the Trinity Lane church in Nashville while I was at Jackson Park church nearby. He also was a student whom I met while in college.

• **Basil Overton** (1926–2013) was preaching at the time for the Southside church in Lexington, Kentucky. He said, "I write poetry on the news of the death of friends at times. Some of these I read at funerals, and others I give to members of the family." He attended the Mars Hill church while I preached there from 1998–2006. He will be 86 on Dec. 3, and now lives with his daughter in Anniston, Alabama.

• **Paul M. Tucker** (1914–2000) was preaching for the Wingate Church of Christ in Nashville, Tennessee. He thought sharing such lessons was "an excellent idea" and would fill "a great need."

• **Fred B. Walker** preached for the Grandview Heights church in Nashville when he sent his lessons. He thought some things preachers might give attention to when assisting a family during the time of a death were: Preparing an obituary to read at a service, having a prior prayer with them, and thinking about how often to visit the family after learning of the death but prior to the service.

•**James W. Watkins, Jr.** (1926–2022) was preaching at East Chattanooga, Tennessee, when he submitted lessons, but has lived in Lewisburg, Tennessee, more recently and is still active in doing meetings and television work.

• **Jess M. Wilcoxson** (1918–2002) preached for the Rose Hill church in Texarkana, TX at the time he sent his lessons. He had just made a move to Texarkana and was apologetic for being delayed in sending them! That was not much of a delay, compared to my delay in getting them in print!

Jack Wilhelm

Blessed Are the Dead

Jim Bill McInteer

Then I heard a voice from heaven, saying to me, Write: Blessed are the dead who die in the Lord from now on. Yes, says the Spirit, that they may rest from their labors and their works follow them (Revelation 14:13).

Therefore, my beloved brethren, be steadfast, unmoveable, always abounding in the work of the Lord, knowing that your labor is not in vain in the Lord (1 Corinthians 15:58).

I. Some Things You Do Not Expect Together:

- A. Pink and Red
- B. July and Snow
- C. Desert and Vegetation.

II. May I Add Another?

- A. Blessedness and Death!
- B. We know this is true ...
- 1. Because it was a "voice from heaven." It was a voice of authority! Who?

- 2. "Write": It was to be permanently preserved. The Holy Spirit said so.

III. See The Statement.

- A. The fact of blessedness was stated, and must be believed.
- B. All deaths, however, are not alike, just as all lives are not alike.
- 1. Much preferred to "die in the Lord!." It is not how but where!
- 2. This implies living in Him—in love, obedience, and communion.

IV. A Two-fold Reason Is Told.

- A. May "rest from their labors." There is a "negative happiness": rest after fatigue, suffering, flaws, imperfections, and sin.
- B. Because our works follow us.
- 1. The Lord contemplates the whole duration of man.
- 2. We can enjoy boundless felicity, connection between this life and the next.
- (Recite qualities of his/her life—not that God needs a review; we do.)
- 3. The life we have formerly lived follows; good is not just for here but hereafter.
- 4. Shall a sainted mother see the work of salvation in husband and sons stop? (A sainted husband see the work of salvation in wife and daughters stop?)
- 5. It has been said: "Death is not a terminus of life but an incident in living."

- a. No broken pillar or extinguished torch to mark the grave.
- b. Heaven is not barren inactivity, but faith becomes sight.
- 6. Though "absent from the body" one is "home with the Lord."

V. Conclusion

Let us glorify God in service that we may have this blessedness.

One City Really Is Ours

Jim Bill McInteer

And they continued three years without war between Syria and Israel. And it came to pass in the third year, that Jehoshaphat the king of Judah came down to the king of Israel. And the king of Israel said unto his servants, "Know ye not that Ramoth in Gilead is ours, and we be still, and take it not out of the hand of the king of Syria?" (1 Kings 22:1–3, KJV)

I. May I Tell You a Story?

    A. Three years of peace had passed between Israel and Syria. In the third year, Jehoshaphat, the good and praised king of Judah, came down to visit Ahab, King of Israel. We don't know why—he just went down. (It was dangerous to be friendly with Ahab, but he just went down.) Ahab made a proposal: "Know ye not that Ramoth in Gilead is ours and we be still, and take it not. ..."

- "Still" is an onomatopoetic word like "hush." They would be afraid to talk—perfectly silent lest they be overcome.
- Ahab killed sheep and oxen in abundance and "persuaded" him to go (2 Chron 18:2).

B. If you recall the story, you remember the defeat in spite of
the machinations of Ahab.

II. Happy is the Man Who Doesn't Rely on His Own Power
But Trusts in the Living God.

- A. I have told this story so that you might see the
  contrast between this story and the deceased.
- B. (Relate the life of the Christian from whom you
  are now parted.)

III. Knowing The Frailty Of The Flesh, He Looked To The
Lord.

- A. Herein is the greatest of joys, that we "trust not in
  chariots and horses" but "remember the name of the
  Lord our God" (Psalm 20:7)
- B. Read Psalm 20:5–9.

> *We will rejoice in thy salvation, and in the name of*
>   *our God we will*
> *Set up out banners; the Lord fulfill all thy petitions.*
> *Now know I that the Lord saveth His anointed;*
> *He will hear him from His holy heaven with the*
>   *saving strength of His right hand.*
> *Some trust in chariots, and some in horses; but we*
>   *will remember the name of the Lord our God*
> *They are brought down and fallen; but we are*
>   *risen, and stand upright.*
> *Save, Lord. Let the king hear us when we call.*

- C. 1 Timothy 4:10 "We both labor and suffer
  reproach, because we trust in the living God, who is
  the Savior of all men, especially of those who believe."
- D. John 6:69 "Also we have come to believe and know
  that You are the Christ, the Son of the living God."

- E. Ephesians 1:11–12 "In Him also we have obtained an inheritance, being predestinated according to the purpose of Him who works all things according to the counsel of His will that we who first trusted in Christ should be to the praise of His glory."

As Far As Bethany

Jim Bill McInteer

And He led them out as far as Bethany, and He lifted up His hands and blessed them. Now it came to pass, while He blessed them, that He was carried up into heaven. And they worshipped Him and returned to Jerusalem with great joy, and were continually in the temple, praising and blessing God. Amen. (Luke 24:50–53)

- Respect and awe would fill this house, were we simply standing in the presence of death itself. But the fury of its descent and the evaluation of the one removed heightens the intensity.
- Could I find a story in Jesus's life when similar emotions grip the heart? I believe Luke 24:50–53 does. Shall we see these points of similarity yet stretched over 20 centuries?

I. The Parallel

Locate the incident: After the resurrection, 40 days of appearances, intense teaching, great responsibilities enjoined by the Great Commission, spirits of enthusiasm after the resurrection role and fell.

II. The Similarity

- A. They went as far as they could go: "As far as Bethany." We do so with our loved ones. Friends streamed in here saying, "He did so much—what can I do?" Loving hands in an hour of departure did everything they could.
- B. But we all come to our extremities. Landmarks and charted courses are destroyed.

III. "What Will I Do?"

- A. We see first what Jesus did: "He blessed them." Jesus was doing something for them.
- 1. Just now, our minds are flooded with the things this individual did.
- 2. Some of those things were: (enumerate)
- B. Then they acted: "They worshipped Him, ... returned with great joy" and "were continually in the temple."
- C. Life continued, even more for the Lord. Not like the atheist who had nothing to stick to. We go on "as far as Bethany" ourselves—like to a graduation—but more must come!

IV. Let's Catch The Vision.

- A. Christ the leader, very calm
- B. Blessing and receiving
- C. Majestic departure—to take His blood, send the Spirit, ever to intercede
- D. True disciples worshipped (adoring dedication returned and they were obedient)
- E. The cloud of death caused them to lose heart, but

the cloud of heaven (Acts 1:9) gave them great joy
(Luke 24:53)

What Is Your Life?

James 4:14

A. Harold Kennamer

Many great lessons are learned by contrast. We think more of life at times of death. • Life is interesting and profitable to study. The lives of others: "Psalm of Life." •A wonderful thing: Hard to define: Having life: Here we stand. Without life: There we lie.

I. Origin

- A. From antecedent life—from God.
- B. Original source: "From whom every good gift cometh; the Father of lights"
- C. "Breathed" into man, Genesis 1

II. The Worth, Value

- A. The shortest life is still valuable.
- B. Life is our schoolroom for eternity: Children attend school from 12 to 20 years.
- C. As valuable as eternity. The present life determines eternity.
- 1. The parable of the Ten Virgins (Matt 25:1–13)

-     2. Sowing for an eternal harvest (Matt 25:46, Gal 6:8–9)
- D. Some are preparing for resurrection but some for condemnation (John 5:28–29, Heb 11:35)
- E. While making preparation, live life the fullest possible, but widening it and expanding it into more abundant life (John 10:10).

III. Life's Phases

- A. What is it retrospectively? ●What has your life been? ●Are you satisfied with it?
-     Take an inventory. Has the past been wasted?
-     Have you been a faithful husband, wife, father, mother, son, daughter, Christian?
- B What is your life introspectively? ●What are you now? ●Are you what you pretend to be? ●Are you satisfied with it? ●Is it being wasted or utilized? ●Are you honest? Truthful? Just? Good? A Christian? ●Are you right with man and God? ●Are you big enough to face yourself?
- C. What are you prospectively? ●What is it for the future? ● Money? ●Fame? ●Pleasure? ●Possessions?
- D."To live is Christ" (Phil 1:21).
- E. "To die is gain" (Phil 1:21).

IV. Life is Brief

- A. A vapor (Jas 4:14) for a "little time." ●Like the morning mist that mantles a mountain (Ps 103:45)
- B. A feast, transient compared to life of God (Ps 90:4)
- C. A "few days" (Job 14:1–2) ●Was said when men lived long
- D. "As a sigh" (Ps 90:9, 12)
- E. As grass (1 Pet 1:24–25)

- F. "For a moment" (2 Cor 4:17) •Benefits of afflictions

V. Life is uncertain but death is certain (Heb 9:27) • Know not the sorrow (Prov 27:1)

VI. An Open Record Before God (Eccl 12:14, 2 Cor 5:10, Heb 4:13–14)

Life and Death

Psalm 1:1–10

A. Harold Kennamer

We have met in the solemnity of this hour to erect monuments of immortal memories that have been engraved in our hearts by the deceased. Monuments are varied and numerous.

Today, we look upon two great mysteries: life and death. Neither can be defined or explained. ●Life is but a short journey from the cradle to the tomb. ●Death must soon be experienced by those of all nations. The living have never experienced it; the dead have never revealed its profound secret.

I. WHAT CAN WE KNOW ABOUT DEATH?

- A. Death Knows No Tender Tie And Values No Earthly Veneration. It comes to: ●the lofty and the low ●the gifted and the rude ● the righteous and the wicked ●the philanthropist and the misanthrope ●the sire and the son. All must bow to the king of terror and go down "to the house appointed for all living."

- B. Death Is Universal: "The youth in life's green spring, and he who goes in the full strength of years, matron and maid, and the sweet babe, the gray-headed man shall, one by one, be gathered to thy side

by those who in their turn shall follow them."
(Bryant)

- C. Death Is Our Mortal Appointment.
-     1. Hebrew 9:27
-     2. Job 30:23 "For I know that You will bring me to death and to the house appointed for all the living." "I must go the way of all the earth."
-     3. Death is not something that "just happens," an unforeseen accident; not something left out in the great scheme of life; but a well-ordered incident and appointment.
-     4. It is not an accident that terminates life or destroys the plan of life, but a turn in the road that sweeps to the illimitable future.
- D. Death Is A Departure. "Jesus knew that His hour had come that He should depart from this world to the Father ..." (John 13:1). The soul does not cease; is not annihilated; cease to communicate in other clime, under other conditions (Jas 2:26, Eccl 8:8)
- E. We Know That We Shall Die
-     1. Eccl 9:5 "For the living know that they will die ..."
-     2. 1 Cor 15:21 "For since by man came death, ... as in Adam all die, even so in Christ all shall be made alive." See Job. 34:15
-     3. The deaths we observe of others is proof: dying daily, every moment.
-     4. From what we feel (observe) in ourselves: ●Life is progressive, as we pass rapidly from one state to another. Some have gone through infancy and youth; others have left in the bloom of life; others have entered old age. ●Loss of sight, hearing, agility and strength are certain notices of approaching dissolution.

II. CONTRARY WINDS COME OUR WAY: MATTHEW 14:22–33

- A. Adverse winds can come. See v. 24: "But the boat was now in the middle of the sea, tossed by the waves for the wind was contrary." In life, adverse winds blow upon every community, every home, and every individual. Are they simply chilling and killing, or can we find in them some kindly meaning?
- B. Occasionally, we are sent into adverse winds: "Jesus made His disciples get into the boat and go before Him to the other side, while He sent the multitudes away" (Matt 14:22). Is there some purpose behind them? Do they represent fate or the Father? If fate, there is no explanation. But IF we learn to say "Our Father" in the storm, then we shall meet a wisdom wiser than the intellect can conceive, a kindness more tender than the imagination can dream.
- C. Adverse winds can come while we are doing our duty. They came to some who were doing what they were "constrained to do": ●Daniel ●Stephen ●Paul ●Mary.
- Being a good person does not immunize one from trouble. Tender hearts may be more easily broken—but they may be more quickly healed.
- D. Adverse winds can be of use.
- 1. They can disclose our special work. Through the storm, Peter found the utterance and leadership he needed that served him well at Pentecost (v. 28).
- a. The death of little Harold McCormick, a grandson of John D. Rockefeller, moved Mr. Rockefeller to establish a hospital for the study of children's diseases, so saving the lives of hundreds of thousands of children later.

-     b. In memory of their lost boy, Mr. and Mrs. Nathan Straus began the distribution of pasteurized milk to the perishing babies of New York.
-     2. Adverse winds develop our strength.
-     a. Peter's faith was strengthened: Matt. 14:30–33, "Then those who were in the boat came and worshiped Him, saying, 'Truly You are the Son of God'."
-     b. England's journeys and discoveries to the frozen lands of the North hardened her mariners for the work of defeating the Spanish Armada.
-     3. Adverse winds can bring to us our richest vision of the Christ. "In the fourth watch of the night, Jesus went to them, walking on the sea." (14:25). The disciples first feared that "it is a ghost!" Jesus spoke words of cheer to them and they were calmed, eventually acknowledging, "Truly, You are the Son of God!" (v. 33).

III. WHAT SHALL WE DO?

- A. Keep on rowing! Do your duty! Live!
- B. Remember that Jesus sees! Mark 6:47–50 "When evening came, the boat was in the middle of the sea; and He was alone on the land. Then He saw them straining at rowing, for the wind was against them. Now about the fourth watch of the night, He came to them, walking on the sea. ... He talked with them and said to them, 'Be of good cheer! It is I; do not be afraid!'"
- C. Let Jesus Calm the Adverse Winds: Matt 14:32

> *God has not promised skies always blue,*
> *Flower-strewn pathways all our life through.*
> *God has not promised sun without rain,*

Joy without sorrow; peace without pain.
But God has promised strength for the day,
Rest for our labor; light for the day.
Grace for the trial; help from above;
Unfailing sympathy; undying love.

Funeral for a Child

Matthew 18:1–6, 10–14

A. Harold Kennamer

When the Lord wanted to teach a lesson on humility, He picked up a child. His estimate of greatness differs wholly from that current among men. •He praised John the Baptist (Matt 11:11), yet said even the least in the kingdom was greater than John. •Jesus gave the illustration of that greatness by a child, which was the clearest picture He could paint for the disciples.

After referring to "little ones in Matthew 18:10, in Matthew 18:14, Jesus said, "It is not the will of your Father who is in heaven that one of these little ones should perish." We are not told how these spirits prosper and mature in the other world. Could it be like a child that has been away to school, under the very best training, for a long time? We wonder just how they will be when they return.

Elliott has expressed some appropriate thoughts along that line:

> He is not dead, the child of our affection,
> But gone into that school
> Where he no longer needs our poor protection.
> But Christ Himself doth rule
> In that great cloister's stillness and seclusion,

By guardian angels led,
Safe from temptation, safe from sin's pollution,
He lives, whom we call dead.

I. THERE IS MITIGATION FOR GRIEF

- A. We may come boldly to the throne of grace (Heb 4:16) "Let us therefore come boldly to the throne of grace, that we may obtain mercy and find grace to help in time of need."
-     1. The same Jesus who spoke pityingly to a distressed mother at the gate of Nain (Luke 7:11–16) is close at hand, able to wipe away tears and lead unto fountains of living waters.
-     2. The same Jesus who wept at the tomb of Lazarus (John 11:35) is "touched with the feeling of our infirmities" (Heb 4:15).
-     3. Psalm 30:5 "Weeping may endure for a night, but joy comes in the morning."
-     4. The rainbow of hope spans the darkness of the grave, as echoing words ring clear: "Suffer the little children..." (Matt 19:14).
- B. Look at it from the child's standpoint.
-     1. As if the picture were reversed and the child were looking back at us: ●We see it garnered safely from the trials of earth. ● Never a generation faced more impending dangers than now. That thought may hold the greatest comforts and joys of suffering. ● The child's angel that beheld the face of God may want to smile with contentment: "To mourn is human; to rejoice divine."
-     2. The child is a full sharer in the bliss of saved immortals. ●If the veil were removed for one moment, we could see the condition of the saved and

safe in Paradise and tears of mourning would flow
more freely as tears of joy.

> *I cannot tell to what sweet dell*
> *The angels have borne thee.*
> *But this I know—thou canst not go*
> *Where my heart will fail to find thee.*

II. THE TENDER SHEPHERD'S CARE

- A. This thought is suggested by Isaiah 40:11 "He will feed His flock like a shepherd; He will gather the lambs with His arm and carry them in His bosom, and gently lead those who are with young."
- B. Two personalities are represented here: One of singularity and the other of a multiplicity. ●One symbolizes unbounded strength and protection. ●The other unmerited, unparalleled weakness and absolute need.
- C. Four words in the text describe what happens: ●(1) Activity: He "gathers them" to shield them from evil, to remove the sore trials that we must bear, to take it out of harm's way and to shield it from impending calamity. ●(2) Strength suggests: power to raise the dead, close the lion's mouth, open the prison and forgive sins. He gathers the lambs in His arms and transfers them to the Heavenly fold. The little rosebud that just begins to open will bloom fully there. What can disturb them? ●(3) Protection: They shall be carried. When a child is lost, then found, it is pressed in his mother's breast and caressed. When Jesus carries them, they never stray. ●(4) Rest suggests a poem by Longfellow:

> *There is a Reaper whose name is Death*

And with his sickle keen,
He reaps the bearded grain at a breath
And the flowers that grow between.
There is no flock, howsoever tended,
But one dead lamb is there.
There is no fireside, howsoe'er defended
But has one vacant chair.

- D. Jeremiah 31:15–17 It was the will of God that many homes be broken that Jesus should live. He now lives, that all broken homes may be healed.

III. LESSONS FROM THE LIFE AND DEATH OF A CHILD

- A. A little life is not wasted. Having begun to live, it is unquenchable. It is guiltless of transgression and enters eternity to begin an endless career.
- B. A child has been your benefactor. ●It taught self-denial and patience, which is the essence of the religion of Jesus. ●It taught to love littleness, feebleness, and helplessness. (See Jas 4:14) Tennyson said: "Twas better to have loved and lost than never to have loved at all." ●We are richer for having a child now safe, beckoning us now onward and upward, purifying a memory of one sacred, sanctified month.
- C. A child is an investment. ● Formerly, we had faith, hope, and confidence and Heaven was then an intangible reality. Though, by nature, heaven must remain intangible as long as we are incarcerated in this flesh, we now have the heart's choicest treasure in the city which hath foundations. Our hearts will be where the treasure is and keep drawing us to go there.
●Formerly, we thought of Heaven as the abode of the faithful patriarchs: Abraham, Isaac, Jacob, Moses,

Joseph, the worthy apostles Peter, James, and John, and persevering saints. Now, we think of it as a natural abode of your own immortalized flesh and blood.

- D. We are led to think of the other world. •We think of the evil your little one escaped. •We think of what future development will be. Here, we can't visualize a giant oak in an acorn or a beautiful flower in a seed. So what will God make of a babe? •We think that Heaven has a new ecstasy. From Heaven must ever come a voice of eloquent entreaty to all left behind, saying, "Meet me there in joy and peace beyond measure!"

The Bible Definition of Death

Psalm 90, Ecclesiastes 12:1–7

Eugene W. Clevenger

Introduction:

●Life is a mystery; eternity is a mystery (Cf. 1 John 3:2); and death is a mystery. ● Much misunderstanding and superstition exist regarding death: ● Regarding what it is. Some say annihilation. ● Regarding why we must die. ● Regarding how the living should react to death. Some celebrate in a festive manner (eat and drink); others are wholly passive and stoical at death; others are bitter. ● We are not interested in speculation and guesses, but in true knowledge of death. This comes only from God's Word.

I. DEATH IS AN APPOINTMENT WITH GOD.

- A. Scriptures which tell us this: Ecclesiastes 3:2, Job 7:1, Job 30:23, Hebrews 9:27
- B. As an appointment of God, it suggests:
- 1. It is not an accident but in God's plan. (The devil introduced death, but God cushions it for Christians.)
- 2. It is not something unprovided for, but He has made provisions for it.
- 3. Not a tragedy, but a well-ordered incident.

- C. Everyone must keep this appointment: •Rich or poor •black or white •good or bad •religious or un-religious, etc.

II. DEATH IS A DEPARTURE FROM THIS LIFE

- A. Scriptures which tell us this (Phil 1:23ff, 2 Tim 4:6)
- B. As a departure from this life, it suggests:
-    a. It can be viewed as the beginning of a journey, a setting sail, a breaking camp.
-    b. A transition from one place to another, from earth to either heaven or hell.
-    c. Suggests the need for careful preparation
-    •Cf. A voyage to Europe means foresight, planning, taking all necessities
-    • Departure of death suggests the most careful planning in life that we do for anything. • Life's main task is to prepare for death because if unprepared for this journey, there is no hope for us. • Heaven is a "prepared place for a prepared people."

III. DEATH IS AN AVENUE TO ETERNAL REST FOR THE PREPARED

- A. Scriptures which tell us this: Revelation 14:13, Hebrews 4:9
- B. Death is a release:
-    1. From the toils of life. "Rest from labors"
-    2. From the burden of sin. We enjoy this release now to some extent (Matt 11:28–30), but completely and perfectly after a while.
-    3. From all the consequences of sin: Worry, grief, sorrow, sadness, pain, etc.

- C. But the pre-requisite is that we must "die in the Lord." This suggests:
-     1. We must get into the Lord. How? Obedience to the gospel (Gal 3:26–27)
-     2. We must remain in the Lord unto death (Matt 10:22, Rev 2: 7, 10).

Conclusion

    What will death mean to me? •An appointment—Will I be prepared to meet it? • A Departure—Where will it take me? Am I making preparation for this all-important journey? • An avenue to eternal rest if we are in the Lord and are abiding in Him. Let us all live in such a way as not to be afraid nor ashamed to meet the Lord in death. As one poet said: "So live that when thy summons comes to join. ..." (*Thanatopsis* by Bryant)

Comfort to Parents on the Death of a Baby

2 Samuel 12:15–23, Romans 8:28, 35–39

Eugene W. Clevenger

I. OUR PURPOSE IN BEING HERE

- A. We are here to sympathize and comfort these parents and this family.
- B. We are not here to answer the question, "Why?" Nobody knows why some are born in perfect health and others are not.
- C. [Jesus did teach that we should not infer that such is an inherited penalty of any kind. (John 9:3)]

II. WHAT ATTITUDE SHOULD WE TAKE WHEN SUCH SORROW COMES?

- A. Certainly not indifference. One of the great blessings of Bible teaching is that we are to treasure the sanctity of life and never view it flippantly. Sadly, in this world some might not care who do not want children very strongly or who do not treasure them.
- B. Not bitterness toward God. God is not responsible for introducing death into the world. It was not in

His planning from the beginning. The "devil sows the tares" in life (Matt 13:39).

- C. Our attitude must be one of faith.

> *O, for a faith that will not shrink*
> *Though pressed by every foe;*
> *That will not trimble on the brink*
> *Of any earthly woe.*
> *That will not murmur nor complain,*
> *Beneath the chastening rod,*
> *But in the hour of grief or pain*
> *Will lean upon its God.*

(Carl Glaser)

III. FACTS THAT WILL HELP US TO UNDERSTAND AND BEAR OUR SORROW

- A. God, our Father, knows, cares and loves. "The eyes of the Lord are over the righteous and His ears are open unto their prayers." (1 Peter 3:12, a quote from Psalm 34:15 that had comforted those in sorrow for centuries.)
- B. There are some things worse than death. •Sin. Babies who die young are spared the struggles with temptation and sin. • Suffering. Going on to be in the presence of God is far better than living a long life of suffering.
- C. The Christian can profit in some way from all experiences of life, even if they are accompanied by pain and sorrow. All accountable people can be reminded of the certainty of death and the necessity of preparation.

On the Death of a Christian Who Suffered Much

Eugene W. Clevenger

I. THE PASSING OF THIS CHRISTIAN MAN MEANS A GREAT LOSS

- A. Loss to the business world. He was a gentleman, fair and honest in all dealings.
- B. Loss to the community. He was a citizen of first rank, interested in his community.
- C. Loss to the home. He was a good husband and loving father, deeply devoted to his family (Eph 5:25, 6:4).
- D. Loss to the church. He was a Christian, zealous, loyal, consecrated, pure—and really could be described by every adjective that describes a faithful Christian. He sought the church first (Matt 6:33). He was willing to spend and be spent. He let his light shine brightly.

II. WHAT SHOULD OUR ATTITUDE BE AS WE THINK OF HIS DEATH?

- A. We should realize that we cannot keep our loved ones with us here forever. We would like to, but reality tells us that we cannot. Death is no respecter of persons.
- B. Realize that in many ways, he is far better off (Phil 1:23, Rev 21:4).
- C. Realize that we must submit to the will of God. God knows best. We are reminded that, "the Lord gives and the Lord takes away. ..."
- D. Realize that death is but a departure to a better land (2 Tim 4:6).
- E. Realize that one day we will be reunited with Him (1 Thess 4:13–18). I want to live in heaven with him and all the redeemed.

May God's richest blessings rest on all of his beloved family members who survive (wife, children and other family members and loved ones). May we all live in this life to be with him in the life which is to come.

DEATH—THE BELIEVER'S POSSESSION

1 CORINTHIANS 3:21–23

EUGENE W. CLEVENGER

The text passage teaches the wealth of the Christian: "All things are yours!"

There are two views of wealth: ● The world's view (the rich men in Luke 12 and Luke 16) and ●the Christian's view: (2 Cor 8:9, 6:10). We can be "rich toward God."

Notice the Christian's heritage, the evidences of God's goodness:

- Christians were blessed by having Paul, Apollos, and Cephas as teachers, friends, and brethren.
- They had the world with its opportunities for service.
- They have life with its blessings and privileges, which is valuable to all who believe.

Then Paul mentions death as a possession of the believer. It is usually regarded as the worst thing of all: a calamity, a curse, a monster, or the grim reaper. Yet Paul calls it a precious possession.

I. DEATH IS OURS AS A REMINDER

- A. It reminds us of the brevity of life.

-     1. We are prone to forget this. Many act as though they will live forever.
-     2. James 4:14, 1 Peter 1:24
- B. It reminds us of the immortality of the soul.
-     1. Nearly all men have believed in immortality. Job asked, "If a man die, shall he live again?" and Paul answered, "For if in this life only we have hope in Christ, we are of all men most miserable."
-     2. Read 1 Corinthians 15:51–57. We will be given immortal bodies to go with our immortal souls.
- C. It reminds us of God's love and goodness (Rom 8:28). God in love calls His redeemed ones home.

II. DEATH IS OURS AS A DISCIPLINE

- A. All need discipline. "All we, like sheep, have gone astray." Death tends to bring us back to right thinking and right deeds.
- B. Death disciplines us, in that:
-     1. It restrains us from sin. We find it difficult knowingly to sin immediately after a funeral, and it ought to be a continual restraint.
-     2. It impresses upon us the folly of the life of sin. No hope for the sinner at death—lost!
-     3. It constrains us to draw closer to God. The song: "Draw Me Nearer"
-     4. It strengthens and encourages us and prepares us for heaven.

III. DEATH IS OURS AS THE AVENUE ONE DAY TO A HAPPIER, NOBLER LIFE

- A. Death is simply the transition from this life to a heavenly life. A change from one state to another (John 14:1–3, Phil 1:21).

- B. Death for the Christian is a release from earth stains and earth pains. The hope of eternal life has removed the sting of death (1 Cor 15:54ff).
- C. As our possession and heritage, death ought not to be feared by the Christian. Only the unprepared need fear it.

Conclusion

1. "And you are Christ's, and Christ is God's." Death is ours only if we are Christ's.
2. We are Christ's (His servants and His possession) only if w are Christians. Everything depends upon whether we are Christians.

THE SHEPHERD PSALM
PSALM 23

BASIL OVERTON

Without this Psalm, how much poorer the world would have been! What a service it has rendered for 3000 years! Think of the comfort and warmth it has shed at funerals.

It is thought that this Psalm was written by David, not in youth, but in old age when he knew the Shepherd well. ● Paraphrase: "I am the sheep's shepherd; the Lord is my shepherd."

There is an interesting story: A young man read the 23rd Psalm excellently. He was praised for his ability to read. Then an old man read the same Psalm and the audience wept. The young man then said, "I know the Psalm, but he knows the Shepherd."

I. 'THE LORD IS *MY* SHEPHERD"

- A. The word "shepherd" is a homely word.
- B. "My shepherd ..." Compare poor children passing a nice house and saying: "This is a pretty house" with other children who would say, "That is our house."
- C. Suppose the Psalm had said: "The Lord is a shepherd." Some must read it that way!
- D. Everyone has all of Christ that he wants. The more one gives of him, the more he has. He is that kind of shepherd!

II. "I SHALL NOT WANT"

- A. Philippians 4:19, 1 Peter 5:7, Matthew 6:33
- B. We cannot say "I shall not want" unless we have taken Christ as the guide in our lives. Neither can we say the Lord is our shepherd.
- C. David did not say, "I have much gold and goods, therefore, I shall not want," even though he was a rich king.
- D. The rich can enter heaven if they use their riches properly and trust in God instead of their riches (1 Tim 6:17–18).

III. "HE RESTORETH MY SOUL"

- A. Note Psalm 19:7 and see how he does this. Compare Romans 1:16.
- B. Though the outward man perishes daily, the inward man is made new (2 Cor 4:16).

IV. "HE LEADETH ME IN THE PATHS OF RIGHTEOUSNESS"

- A. Eastern shepherds lead; they do not drive.
- B. The Lord leads and draws. He does not drive. Note how He does this: John 6:44–45.

Conclusion

Try to contemplate dwelling in the "house of the Lord forever." This hope alone makes our duties seem as nothing and our trials but for a little while (2 Cor 4:17–18, 1 Pet 5:10).

This Psalm has contributed much to the world. One man said he would rather have written this Psalm than to have built the Pyramids! This Psalm has meant far more to the world than the Pyramids have.

(Closing remarks as may seem appropriate.)

POEMS
BASIL OVERTON

In Memory of a Friend

Big enough to be brave,
To build in spite of flay of foe;
Like a Marathon General he clave
To his task, blow by blow.

With lifting words he often said
To younger ones like me:
"You can move ahead
In the work of making men free."

Not from Hellas did ever one so great
March in battle strong arrayed
Like him, who with his mate
Served others undismayed.

Friend to all, who would suffer him so,
But, more than a friend to those
Bereft of home where love doth flow.
For those he toiled as only God knows.

———

To A Noble Man

His heart was set on noble things:
Virtue, piety, truth and love;
Always seeking the goal that brings
One in touch with God above.

Not for self was his effort made,
Nor for praise of fellow men;
But for the reward that does not fade
He spent his little life span.

We weep, not as if no hope
Were ours to embrace,
But we rejoice in limited scope,
And depend on His undying grace.

———

An Ode to a Friend

Not for gold was she my friend,
Nor for riches vain;
But for love of Jesus she would bend
Her efforts for my gain.

Christ's messenger needs an encouraging word
To bolster him in his sacred task.
From her I often heard

More than I could ask.

Lord, relieve us of our complaints;
May all submit to Thy Holy Will
And know that precious is the death of thy saints,
In Thine eyes, it is so still.

———

Remember

Success, as measured by man,
May bear the stamp of wealth;
But God has another plan
And measures by the soul's health.

Life can be a season of sowing seeds;
Seeds of kindness, grace and truth,
Or a time of wasted years and deeds,
But wisdom cries: "Remember God in youth!"

Nor for self alone was he serene and kind,
But that we his friends might see
The meaning of Christ, and find
In Him the truth that sets men free.

To this loved one we say, "So long."
Only for a time will be the night
Without his smile, the gentle voice and song
Of one gone on seraphic flight.

WHO ARE THE DEAD?

BASIL OVERTON

We often speak of "the dead." What do we mean?

There are different senses in which the term "dead" is used in the Bible and in our conversations:

- We speak of the dead physical bodies who are placed in the various kinds of receptacles for burial (Gen 23:4, Luke 7:12).
- We speak of the dead *in* sin. They are the living dead! (Matt 8:22, 1 Tim 5:6, Luke 15:24)
- We speak of the dead *to* sin. Those who are free from sin as a slave master (Rom 6:1–6, Col 1:2, Col 3:3).
- We speak of the dead, meaning those spirits whose dwelling place has been in human bodies (Luke 16:30, Rev 14:13). In a sense, these are alive: They are conscious (Rev 6:9–11, 2 Cor 12:1–4).
- These dead we call "souls." But the word "soul" is used in the Bible in different senses:
- It can be a whole person (Rom 13:1; Acts 7:14, 2:41–43; 1 Pet 3:20).
- It can be animal life; physical life (Gen 2:7, Ps 78:50). In Genesis 2:7, "living soul" is from Hebrew

terminology that was applied to animals also, as in Genesis 1:20, 21, 24, etc. where it is translated as "living creature."
- It can be "inner man," or "spirit" (Acts 2:27, 3 John 2, Dan 7:12, Matt 10:28, 2 Cor 4:16).

Conclusion

- At a funeral is a good time for us to ponder the question: "Where will my soul be when my body is lying before a funeral speaker and before a crowd of friends and loved ones?"
- Surely the deceased would say, if he/she could speak to us: "I am glad you are reminding the living of their responsibility with respect to the destiny of their immortal souls."
- (Use whatever closing words that may be appropriate for the occasion.)

The Resurrection of the Dead

Basil Overton

Resurrection! What a wonderful word to use at a funeral. All should be thankful that we can talk about the resurrection of the dead when death has lowered its dark cloud upon our hearts.

- If death were an eternal gorge of gloom; if there were no escape from the cold dust of death; if the grave were an eternal prison house—how different we would feel.
- The New Testament speaks in one way or another of the Second Coming of Christ about 300 times. This is an average of about once every 20th verse. He is coming again! And one of the things He is going to do is raise the dead.

I. CHRIST IS THE "FIRST FRUITS OF THEM THAT SLEPT." (1 Cor 15:20)

- The "firstborn of every creature" (Col 1:15).
- "Firstborn from the dead" (Col. 1:28).
- "First begotten of the dead" (Rev 1:5).

- How may we reconcile these statements with the fact that others were raised from the dead before Christ was? (1 Kgs 17, 2 Kgs 4, Matt 9, Luke 7, John 11).
- Paul gave the answer to the above question at Antioch in Pisidia: "And concerning that He raised Him up from the dead, now no more to return to corruption" (Acts 13:33–35).
- Jesus was the first to be raised not to die again; the first to be raised in the manner that all will be raised on the last day.

II. WHAT OF THE RESURRECTION OF ALL THE DEAD?

- Raised with immortal bodies (1 Cor 15:35, 42–44–58)
- A glorious body like unto Christ's (Phil 3:21)
- We shall be like Him when we see Him as He is (1 John 3:1–2)
- All will be raised at the same time (John 5:28–29)
- Faithful will be raised to life eternal (John 5:28–29)
- Unrighteous will be raised to eternal damnation (John 5:28–29)

III. WHAT OF THOSE LIVING AT THE TIME OF THE RESURRECTION OF THE DEAD?

- They shall not have preference over the dead. The dead shall be raised before the righteous that are alive shall go to be with the Lord. The dead shall be raised first! (1 Thess 4:13–18).
- The living shall be changed from mortal to immortal in a moment, in the twinkling of an eye (1 Cor 15:50–54).

Conclusion

- Hope is the anchor of the soul (Heb 6:19).
- Some shall not have this anchor (1 Thess 4:13)
- (Add remarks that seem appropriate for the particular occasion.)

The Challenge of Noble Womanhood

On the Death of a Saintly Lady:
Proverbs 31:10–31

Paul M. Tucker

Solomon's description of a worthy woman is a challenge. I believe this saintly Christian lady whose memory we honor today was a rare, precious worthy woman. What does this mean as a challenge to those of us who survive?

I. A WORTHY WOMAN IS PRICELESS IN VALUE

- A. There are many women in this world today, but a virtuous, worthy woman is rare.
- B. The commercial value of a commodity is largely determined by supply and demand. The supply of worthy women today is very limited. The demand should be great. She is rare!
- C. Proverbs 31:10 "Her price is far above rubies." This good woman today has left riches to her family —namely, a precious hope that is in their hearts.
- D. She has left a "good name," which also is priceless (Prov 22:1).
- She has left honor to her husband (Prov 31:23).

- Her challenge to us is to live lives worthy of that worthy name and precious heritage that she has left us.

II. A WORTHY WOMAN IS NOT AFRAID OF THE FUTURE

- A. "She is not afraid of the snow ..." (Prov 31:21).
- B. "She laughs at the time to come ..." (Prov 31:25 RSV).
- C. Why is she not afraid?
- 1. She has prepared (note references in several verses).
- 2. We are taught to prepare to meet God (Amos 4:12).
- 3. Heaven is a prepared place for a prepared people (John 14:1–6).
- D. She could apply Psalm 23 with confidence to her future. Her challenge to us is to prepare as she did, so that we, too, can approach death with confidence.

III. A WORTHY WOMAN FEARS JEHOVAH

- A. This is commendable, Proverbs 31:30 "A woman who fears the Lord, she shall be praised."
- B. This is the whole duty of man (Eccl 12:13)
- C. This trait calls for respect, reverence for, and obedience to God's law.
- D. Her challenge to us is to develop such recognition for God's law, the Bible.

IV. HER REWARD—PRAISE FROM HER CHILDREN AND HUSBAND

- A. Both praise her (Prov 31:28). This is more than mere lip service. She deserved the praise of all of her family.
- B. Her challenge to us is to honor her and praise her by a life of service to others and to the glory of God, rather than to reproach her worthy name by lives of disobedience.

V. HER ABIDING INFLUENCE OF HER NOBLE EXAMPLE

- A. "Let her works praise her" (Prov 31:31) Her works speak louder than her words.
- B. With all of us: "Their works do follow them" (Rev 14:13)
- C. Her challenge to us in this respect is to emulate her example of doing good, in faith and good works.

Conclusion

May we accept her challenge, receive the torch, and faithfully pass it on to others.

———

I know it is over, over,
I know it is over at last!
Down sail! The sheathed anchor uncover,
For the stress of the voyage is past.

Life, like a tempest of ocean,
Hath out-sheathed its ultimate blast.
There's but a faint sobbing seaward,
While the calm of the tide deepens leaward,

And behold! Like the welcoming quiver

Of heart-pulses throbbing through the river,
Those lights in the harbor at last,
The heavenly harbor at last!

— AUTHOR UNKNOWN, SUBMITTED BY
PAUL M. TUCKER

CHRIST'S COMFORTS

1 THESSALONIANS 4:13–17, JOHN 14:1–6

PAUL M. TUCKER

In this world, we have many needs, one of which is comfort. God's Word supplies all our needs. Notice 1 Thessalonians 4:18 and also Christ's words in John 14:1–6.

There are some things Jesus asked His disciples to believe that would bring comfort to them after He left them:.

I. HE ASKED THEM TO AFFIRM THAT "YOU BELIEVE IN GOD" (John 14:1)

- A. Jesus's disciples were in great distress then.
- B. There is no comfort possible apart from an intelligent belief in God.
- C. Christ did not here prove God's existence; He assumed that belief.
- D. Christ did not come to reveal the existence of God, but the nature, characteristics and the fatherhood of God (John 10:30, Acts 17:26).
- E. Remove faith in the existence and fatherhood of God, and we have no ground for hope.

II. HE ASKED THEM TO "BELIEVE ALSO IN ME" (John 14:1)

- A. Faith in Jesus as God's Son is indispensable.
- B. Jesus is the "light of the world" (John 8:12). (Light dispels darkness, fear, etc.)
- C. Jesus is the "water of life" (John 4:14). (An essential for life to exist.)
- D. Jesus is our Savior (Acts 4:12).
- E. Jesus is the way, the truth, and the life (John 14:6).
- F. Jesus is the resurrection and the life (John 11:25).
-      1. As shown at Lazarus's tomb (John 11:25, 43–44)
-      2. As with the son of the widow of Nain (Luke 7:14–15)
-      3. As in His own resurrection (Rom 1:4)
-      4. As He will be with us all (John 5:28–29)

III. HE ASKED THEM TO BELIEVE THAT "IN MY FATHER'S HOUSE ARE MANY MANSIONS" (John 14:2)

- A. "Mansions" are considered to be costly and elaborate, with much room.
- B. It will be a tabernacle, not made with hands (2 Cor 5:1).
- C. We must prepare for it.

Conclusion

May Christ's comforts to His disciples who were mourning His departure also be yours today.

I SHALL GO TO HIM

2 SAMUEL 12:16–23

PAUL M. TUCKER

The loss is much, the burden is heavy for this family. We rejoice, however, that God gave this child to these parents as long as He did.

Because of what the Bible teaches on the state of a child, we know this family will be represented in heaven, at least by this child (Matt 18:3, 19:14).

I. DAVID'S EXPERIENCE

- A. Note David's prayer and his humiliation (2 Sam 12:16)
- B. It was not God's will that David keep this child.
- C. David's response to the child's death:
- 1. He resumed the normal processes of life (v. 20)
- 2. He went to God's house and worshipped (v. 20)
- 3. He returned to his own house and to the duties of life (v. 20)
- 4. He was submissive to God's will (v. 22, 23)
- 5. He was comforted in his sorrow, and he comforted Bathsheba, the child's mother

- 6. His conviction was: "I shall go to him, but he shall not return" (v. 23)

II. TO WHAT WOULD A CHILD BE BROUGHT BACK, IF SUCH WERE TO HAPPEN?

We have no such power—and would not, if we could, or could not if we would. But to what would a child return, if such were possible?

- A. To a world where temptation and sin abound (Rom 3:9, 23)
- B. To a world of tribulation, trials and wars. "Man's inhumanity to man makes countless millions mourn."
- C. To the problem of growing to maturity and providing a livelihood in a world that is becoming less humane each day.
- D. To a world from which he would again be removed by death. ●Lazarus was raised but had to die again. ●The son of the widow of Nain had to die again. ●All must die (Heb 9:27). ●[Only Christ came back from the dead never to see corruption and death again (Acts 13:34).]
- E. To a world of decay, sickness and death. This is the common lot of all until heaven is a reality (Rev. 21:4, 22:1–5). The human body has been so constituted to weaken and sicken (1 Pet 1:24).

III. "I SHALL GO TO HIM"—WHERE WILL THAT BE?

- A. To the home of the soul. ●Infants are not guilty of any sin, either inherited or committed. The idea of "inherited depravity" and "original sin" is not in the Bible. Infants are as perfect as the angel around God's throne (Matt 18:3, 19:14). ●The church of Christ has stood almost alone in the religious world in proclaiming Bible truth about this doctrine. Infants are not saved because they were never lost; they are safe in the arms of Jesus.

- B. To a mansion prepared for the faithful (John 14:1)
- C. To a house not made with hands (2 Cor 5:1)
- D. To where there will be no tears and sorrows (Rev 21:4, 22:1–5)

Conclusion

Would it really be wise to rob this child of the certainty of his reward to bring him back and make it uncertain? Let us resolve to live so that when we depart, we can "go to this child" with a comforting faith and a rewarding hope.

HE IS NOT HERE BUT RISEN

LUKE 24:1–9

FRED B. WALKER

These words apply to Jesus, but they give us great hope regarding our loved ones.

In many ways, I like to think of this Christian man who has died as having "risen."

I. HE WAS RAISED FROM THE WATERY GRAVE OF BAPTISM.

- A. He was baptized (date), along with others who heard the Gospel at the time.
- B. In doing so, he had a part in the first resurrection (Rev 20:6).
- C. Gospel preachers are always very happy to have a part in assisting those who obey the Gospel, to have a part in the "first resurrection" (Rom 6:4–5).
- D. In Christ, one is raised up to be a new creature (Col 3:1). They are to "abide in Him" (John 15:4–8).

II. HE HAD EARLIER RISEN FROM BABYHOOD TO THE SILL OF MANHOOD

- A. He was proud of his "roots" and his home community.
- B. Early memories of him by all who knew him then will rise continually in your hearts to ease the pang of his leaving.
- C. God raised him up for a purpose—to life a useful life.
- D. As Paul ran a good race, our deceased friend also ran his race (2 Tim 4:1–5). [It has been an established procedure of God to have one in the right place at the right time, as He did with Paul and also with Esther.]

III. HIS SPIRIT HAS RISEN FROM THIS TABER-
NACLE OF FLESH BEFORE US.

- A. Suggestive to us of vapors that rise from the embers of a sacrifice of old
- B. As the essence of nature's raw materials are distilled into spirits rising
- C. [Ecclesiastes 12:7 "Then the dust will return to the earth as it was, and the spirit will return to God who gave it." See James 2:26 also.]

IV. IT CAN BE SAID THAT HE IS RISING AGAIN IN
THE IMAGE OF HIS CHILDREN

- A. [We often hear an expression: "Like father, like son." Observers often will say that they see us in our children, as children exhibit impressions parents have made on them. This is as it should be and is a great asset to humanity when the examples set are as they should be.]
- B. His loved ones have the great blessing of his example.

V. THERE IS THE COMING RESURRECTION OF ALL THE DEAD IN WHICH WE ALL WILL RISE.

- A. Everyone shall be there (John 5:28–29). [See 1 Thess 4:16–18]
- B. The judgment will follow and eternal destinies will be announced (Matt 25:34, 45–46).
- C. We spend our energies more on maintaining physical life here, when it would be much more worthwhile to take pains to assure us of eternal life (Luke 13:34).

Conclusion

Alfred Lord Tennyson's beautiful poem has comforted mourners for well over a century. It still speaks to our hearts today:

Crossing The Bar

Sunset and evening star
And one clear call for me.
And may there be no moaning of the bar
When I put out to sea.
But such a tide, as moving seems asleep,
Too full for sound and foam;
When that which drew from out the boundless deep,
Turns again home, Turns again home.

Twilight and evening bell,
And after that the dark!
And may there be no sadness of farewell
When I, when I embark.
For tho' from out our bourne of Time and Place,

The flood may bear me far.
I hope to see my Pilot face to face,
When I have crossed the bar.

— ALFRED LORD TENNYSON

THE STONE ROLLED AWAY

PSALM 90 OR 91

FRED B. WALKER

(Review the life of the deceased.) We are now in the presence of the chamber of death. We stand beside the mortality of one to whom the gates of death have been opened to let his soul pass within. Doors are forever closing on us. Some of which can never be reopened.

Read Genesis 3:22–24. God set a flaming sword at the entrance of Eden. The gates of death were closed on Jesus at the age of 33. But on the third day, they found the stone rolled away.

I. WHAT DOES THE DEATH OF CHRIST AND RESURRECTION MEAN?

- A. That sin was rolled away.
- 1. Before His death, there was no complete remission. The blood of animals could not take away sin.
- 2. Every sin plunged man deeper into the mire of guilt.
- 3. "Because of the blood of your covenant I will set your prisoners free from the waterless pit" (Zech 9:11).
- B. The fear of death was rolled away.

- 1. Like the magnet mountain in the story, the attraction was irresistible that drew men to their death, or like the call of the sirens in the wanderings of Ulysses.
- 2. One writer: "Every stroke of my heart that I listen to at night sounds to me as the ax of the woodman hacking down the tree of life."
- 3. Death is feared, because it leads to the unknown.
- 4. Goethe, when dying, said in an agitated voice: "What is coming? Oh, it is dark; it is dark!"
- 5. That is the story of the unbeliever: uncertainty, gloom—the stone is on the sepulcher.
- 6. The words of a believer at death: "Oh, how bright!" Said with the affable smile. The stone of fear was rolled away.
- C. The Misery of Separation Was Rolled Away.
- 1. It is a bitter thing for the heathen father to separate from his dying child. No hope.
- 2. All the sweet affection is still in the dead heart forever.
- 3. It is different with a Christian: • "Let not your heart be troubled." • "I am the resurrection and the life." • "Blessed are the dead." • "It is better to depart and be at home with the Lord."

II. WE ALL DO FADE AS A LEAF (Isa 64:6)

- A. Isaiah 64:6 "But we are all as an unclean thing, and all our righteousnesses are as filthy rags; and we all do fade as a leaf; and our iniquities, like the wind, have taken us away."
- B. How like life is the budding leaf in spring, then in full glory in summer. In the autumn the cold wind has touched its heart, chilled the sap, slowed

the circulation. The leaf becomes seared and withered.

- C. Analogies: ●The leaf fades by gradual process. Not by one blast, but a leaf at a time. ●The leaf goes back to its primitive elements. ●It fades to prepare for a new life. ●The seed has to die for new life also (1 Cor 15:25–44).

III. FOUR STATES OF MIND EXIST AS TO THE DEATH OF THE BODY

- A. There is unreasoning indifference: The great masses of mankind are stolidly indifferent. "They deem all men mortal but themselves." Only blind stupidity can cause man to look upon death with complete indifference. "Oh, that men were wise, that they would consider their latter end" (Prov 19:20).
- B. There is intellectual stoicism: That death is just the end of existence. These place the reasoning of men whose philosophy of life and death flash as a bright meteor through the sky but is gone tomorrow against the enduring ROCK OF AGES. Christ, and the Bible, like sunshine, outshines all until the end of time.
-     The intellectuals represent this as a rest to the mind, but how reached? ●By condemning the simple faith by which greater than they have lived and died. ●By quenching our aspirations for another life and destroying our nature's pantings for immortality. ●By condemning the Bible as cunningly devised fables. How few can do this, but even when they do, do they have rest?
- C. There is terrible foreboding: "All their lifetime, subject to fear." They are conscious what death will do to them. "It will take them from their property,

house, friendships, pleasures, and hasten them into a journey for which they are unprepared." Any intimation of dying fills them with terror. ●Is this really a desirable state of mind?

- D. There is Christian composure: Christians look at death with a calm and tranquil spirit. They see triumph in tragedy (Rom 8). ●They have knowledge that what they are experiencing is common to mankind. ● They have happy memories accumulated through the years. ●They have children, grandchildren, and friends who share their hope. ● They anticipate a joyful reunion. ● They view a righteous partner who has gone on as helping them prepare the way for the survivor. The passing of a Christian partner, wife, or husband, is not a separation from God but a view that brings them into closer fellowship with Him. ●Nothing is supremely tragic in this world but separation from God.

Conclusion

This is the message I believe your deceased loved one would want me to leave with you in the family and all who mourn. (He) was a person of great faith and desired that others share that faith. (He) would want you and me to live so as to avoid separation from God.

Comfort One Another

1 Thessalonians 4:13–18

Elvis H. Huffard

I. Introduction

- A. Grief is seldom so great as when we say goodbye to a loved one.
- 1. Enjoyable experiences involving the deceased will come to our minds that will chill us when we realize that they cannot be repeated but will have to be consigned to memories.
- 2. Frequently we will want to relate events to the deceased and will not realize until the second thought that it cannot be done.
- B. God who does all things well has given us a source of comfort in time of grief. We on this funeral occasion can be comforted by His Word.

II. Discussion

- A. Comfort comes from several sources.
- 1. From friends and family expressions of sympathy are extended that help the bereaved immeasurably.

-         a. A firm handshake with no words spoken can mean a great deal.
-         b. Flowers and cards let the bereaved know that there are those who weep with him.
-         c. Such expressions have great value, but they also have their limitations.
-     2. The pleasant memories of the deceased keep them alive and there is great comfort in this.
-     3. It is comforting to know that God can hear us as we cry out in sorrow.
-     4. The greatest comfort comes from God by the resurrection of Jesus Christ. This was the comfort encouraged by Paul to the Thessalonians.
- B. What thoughts were presented by Paul to be used in comforting others? These thoughts are vital in accomplishing the purpose of this gathering today in memory of the deceased (1 Thess 4:13–18).
-     1. If we are believers we have no occasion to sorrow without hope over death.
-         a. Jesus died, but He arose! (Matt 18:6)
-         b. He was victorious over the grave and death (1 Cor 15:57).
-         c. He is going to come again (John 14:3)
-         d. He will bring the saints with Him (John 5:28–29).
-     2. The faithful living will join those gone before (1 Thess 4:17).
-     3. We will ever be with the Lord (John 14:1–3).
- C. Nothing can compare with the comfort given with the full realization of the meaning of the resurrection of Christ.

- 1. Man's universal desire to live on and on is strong.
- 2. Man's desires for beauty, peace, and happiness can be gratified (Rev 21:1–4).

III. Conclusion

- A. Faith in God and His word makes possible comfort in this hour of sorrow.
- B. The living need to live in full view of the comfort we can bring to others through Jesus.

The Christian's View of Death

2 Corinthians 5:1–11

Elvis H. Huffard

I. Introduction

- A. Every accountable person is made aware of death every day.
  - 1. The daily newspaper keeps us informed.
  - 2. Daily Bible reading enlightens all of us (Heb 9:27).
  - 3. Any active person brushes with death daily. Example: Speeding along the highway, the driver just misses death by a few feet with every approaching car.
- B. In view of the certainty of death, people react in several ways.
  - 1. We can completely disregard the possibilities and say, "Others may die, but not me."
  - 2. We can live in great fear of death to the point of curtailing activities and becoming useless.
  - 3. We can give full recognition to the realities of death.

II. Discussion

- A. The Christian looks first to the approach to death: life.
- 1. Through Paul, he sees life as a temporary existence, a tabernacle on earth (2 Cor 5:1–11).
- 2. A recognition of life is made as an enjoyable existence, even if it does have its difficulties, disappointments, and sorrows (Rom 8:28–30).
- 3. Life is directed toward its end on earth and then the judgment (Heb. 9:27, Eccl 12:13, 2 Cor 5:10–11).
- B. The Christian is able to see death realistically. In full recognition of it, he can make life a beautiful existence.
- 1. He sees death as an appointment that all must meet (Heb 9:27).
- 2. He can appreciate the resurrection as it removes the sting of death (1 Cor 15:55–58).
- 3. He has complete victory in Christ (1 Cor 15:57).
- a. There will be no more death (Luke 20:35–36, Rev 21:4).
- b. There will be an existence of eternal joy (Ps 16:11).
- c. There will be companionship with all the saints (Matt 8:11, 19:29).
- d. There will be eventually the realization of everlasting life (Matt 25:46).
- 4. He views death as a step of transition into the morning of joy (1 Cor 15:35–54).

Conclusion

- A. The Christian prepares for death by living for Christ (Amos 4:12).

- B. These thoughts should be of great value as we are made aware of death as we see it in the departed one.

Not Alone in Death

Psalm 23

Elvis H. Huffard

Introduction

- A. There are times in every man's life when he desires to be without human companionship.
- 1. Time spent in serious reflection or meditation demands isolation from things that detract. Moments spent in memory of the deceased could be an example.
- 2. Earnest prayers to God can best be uttered in the closet.
- B. There are times when man as a social being demands human companionship.
- 1. Early in life, one learns to be encouraged by the presence of parents or friends.
- 2. In business, grave decisions are made after consulting others.
- 3. Human companionship and sympathy are appreciated in hours of bereavement.
- 4. Many tasks faced by men remind them of their limitations. In such cases, they do not want to be left alone.

Discussion

- A. There are many things about Death that force men to see their limitations.
- 1. Some day death will end our existence as we experience life (Heb 9:27).
- 2. The immortal will put on immortality (1 Cor 15:54).
- 3. Death is a one-time experience. Therefore, man knows no such repeated experience while living. It is a step that all realize fully: "We walk by faith, and not by sight" (2 Cor 5:7).
- B. The contemplated experience of Death is such that no man desires to face it alone.
- 1. The dying man reaches out his hand to the doctor, nurses, loved ones, or friends to steady him.
- 2. African chiefs of days gone by often left orders for several of their wives to be killed and placed in the grave with his body so as to have company in their last voyage.
- 3. Regardless of how many might surround the dying man, he takes the final step alone without human companionship.
- C. Consoling is the thought allowed to every Christian in knowing that he does not go alone.
- 1. The faith and assurance of the Psalmist can be experienced by the Christian (Ps 23:4).
- a. The Lord is the Christian's Shepherd also.
- b. Fear is removed with the full assurance that the Lord is with the man approaching death.
- 2. The Lord has given many promises and backed them up by the resurrection to assure the Christian that he is not alone, and that he has nothing to fear.

III. Conclusion

- A. The departed one is not alone if he died in the faith. He has departed from the living, but he is safe with the Lord.
- B. All who remain should live with Christ today so as to have Him guide them over the chilly waters of death.

———

"Never Alone"
4th Stanza of the Song

He died for me on the mountain,
For me they pierced His side.
From me He opened that fountain,
The crimson cleansing tide.

For me He's waiting in glory,
Seated by His throne.
He promised never to leave me,
Never to leave me alone.

Chorus
No, never alone,
No, never alone.
He promised never to leave me,
Never to leave me alone.

A Christian's Gains
and Losses in Death
Paul Hunton

Paul said, "It is s better for me to go and be with Christ, but better for you that I remain" (Phil 1:23–24).

I. LOSSES

1. The church has lost a member
2. Business has lost an industrious person
3. The community has lost an upright citizen
4. Children have lost a parent. (Identify other relationships as appropriate ●Parents have lost a child ●A husband has lost his wife ●A wife has lost her husband ●or it may be that some have lost a brother or sister.)

II. GAINS

1. Freedom from physical suffering and deterioration
2. Freed from spiritual enemies
3. Freed from material struggles to exist
4. Freed from death in the future
5. With loved ones who have gone on, while all await our arrival

6. Awaiting happily for the judgment day and eternal joy

I Shall not Want

Psalm 23

Paul Hunton

David had many experiences with God and spoke as an authority. The unbeliever has no right to speak and truly, "The fool has said in his heart, 'There is no God'."

The Bible declares, "I have never seen the righteous forsaken nor His seed begging bread" (Ps 37:25).

We are taught to "Seek the kingdom of God first" (Matt 6:25–34).

From Psalm 23, we learn:

- I. I shall not want for material things: There will be "green pastures" and "still waters" (v. 2).
- II. I shall not want for leadership: "He leadeth me ... (v. 2, 3).
- III. I shall not want for courage: "I will fear no evil ..." (v. 4).
- IV. I shall not want for protection: "Thou preparest a table before me in the presence of mine enemies" (v. 5).
- V. I shall not want for the restoration of my soul: "He restoreth my soul ..." (v. 3).
- Conclusion: "My cup runneth over" (v. 5).

QUESTIONS AT DEATH

PAUL HUNTON

There are many questions for which we seek an answer throughout life. The inquisitive mind of a child, a student, yes, of everyone, is very common. The revealed things belong to man, but God reserves to Himself the unrevealed (Deut 29:29).

At death, there are pertinent and relevant questions.

I. WHAT IS LIFE?

1. Life is like a pilgrimage.
2. Life is a period of activity.
3. Life is a stewardship.
4. Life is a period of preparation.

Note: ● Life is precious and all struggle to live from the lowest form to the highest. ● God is the source of all life.

II. WHAT IS DEATH?

1. Death is an uncovering (1 Cor 3:16–17, 6:19–20).
2. Death is like embarking from one shore where friends and loved ones bid you goodbye to another shore where you will be welcomed.
3. Death is a transition.

Note: •It is not enough to die unafraid. One must think of accountability. • 2 Timothy 4:6–8 explains the close of a successful life.

III. WHAT IS BEYOND?

1. A better life
2. Perfect love
3. Complete liberty
4. Adequate security

Funeral Thoughts for a Christian Woman

James W. Watkins, Jr.

This good Christian lady, as we knew her, was made in the image and likeness of God. That is, as a free moral agent, having the power to do good or evil. In view of this and in consideration of human frailties, she was subject to mistakes. All of us are, even as were godly men of old like David, Peter, etc. Underlying all is the disposition of heart as to whether we are big enough to admit we have sinned.

If we could call our sister back today, we might have a disposition to correct any mistakes we could find, but there are some things we would not change:

I. She had faith in God and in His Son, Jesus. Some may not have faith, but we would not change her faith! We would not have her go through life as an infidel! You know Hebrews 11:6, Romans 10:17.

II. She was penitent. Years ago, she obeyed the first principles of the gospel and repented of her sins. We would not change that if we could and have her walk in sin (Luke 13:3).

III. She confessed Christ. Not only by word of mouth in obedience to those first principles, but she also confessed Christ by her manner of life. We certainly would not change that (Rom 10:9–10, Matt 10:32–33).

IV. She was baptized for the remission of all past sins (Mark 16:15–16, Acts 2:38, Luke 7:29–30).

V. She wore the name of Christ (Acts 11:26, 1 Peter 4:16, Acts 4:11–12).

VI. She worshipped (Heb 10:25). She counted the fellowship of fellow Christians as worthwhile. We would not have her forsake the assembly.

VII. She was satisfied with the Church of Christ. If she were with us again, we would not have her trade that preference for an institution not named in the Bible (Acts 20:28).

VIII. She was kind and benevolent—an observation I made from my own association with her. We would not have her change that. Jesus placed too much importance on such matters (Acts 10:38).

IX. Even on occasions of business, she sought opportunity to teach the truth. She was no "secret disciple," but took advantage of every opportunity to teach.

Conclusion

We say we would not change any of these things in her life, so why not strive to imitate them? Even as Paul said: "Be imitators of me even as I am of Christ" (1 Cor 11:1). To the family, Paul also says: "Sorrow not even as the rest who have no hope." (1 Thess 4).

Funeral Thoughts for a Christian Man

James W. Watkins, Jr.

This is a sad, solemn occasion. Yet necessary to respect for life and sacred things. Time and energy are more profitably spent when dealing with those who are yet alive. We see life as it is lived and we are prone to ask some questions:

I. WHAT IS LIFE? Genesis 2:7

- A. We are made to see its transitory nature: Job 14:1–2, James 4:14, Hebrews 9:27, 2 Samuel 14:14.
- B. Life is uncertain. We need thus to seek security: Acts 20:32, Proverbs 30:5.

II. WE ARE NOT LEFT WITHOUT INFORMATION AND INSTRUCTION

- Scriptures that help us: Hebrews 1:1–2; Matthew 17:5, 7:24

III. JESUS INVITED US TO COME TO HIM. Matthew 11:28

- A. He told us how to do so: John 6:44–45. Stresses the significance of hearing
- B. He told us what to believe and to do:
-     1. Believe in Him as God's Son (John 8:24, Heb 11:6)
-     2. Repent of sins (Acts 17:30,Luke 13:3)
-     3. Confess our faith in Him (Rom 10:10, Matt 10:32)
-     4. Be baptized (immersed) Mark 16:15–16, John 3:5 (to be born again)

IV. PLEASE NOTE: THESE QUOTATIONS HAVE BEEN EXCLUSIVELY FROM THE SON OF GOD!

It was Jesus who identified each of these very important things to do—either to believe or die in sin, either to repent or perish, either to confess or be denied, either to be baptized or to stay out of the kingdom.

(Close with appropriate words to the family.)

Thoughts About Saving Obedience To God

Ecclesiastes 12:1–7

James W. Watkins, Jr.

Solomon depicted Death to us, showing that we must all go soon to our eternal home (Heb 9:27). The one who lived in this tabernacle of clay has departed. Anytime we lose a friend or loved one, it is a reminder to us that ●Life is brief and ●Eternity will be long. Some Scriptures take on more meaning to us on such occasions: ● Job 14:1–2, ● James 4:14, ● 2 Samuel 14:14, and ●1 Peter 1:24.

Some Thoughts That We Should Consider While Time Remains:

- Life is the time for preparation for eternity as we consider our own lives in view of death: ●Romans 3:23, ● Ecclesiastes 7:20, ● Jeremiah 10:23, ● Ephesians 2:12
- When God looked down on the sinful condition of the world, instead of condemning it with an impulsive overthrow, He made possible a way of redemption and escape! ● John 3:16, ● 2 Timothy 1:10, ● Romans 1:16
- Believers are saved by the gospel by obeying it: ● 2 Thessalonians 1:7–9, ● Hebrews 5:8–9

- The New Testament is our only source of information about what one must do in order to "obey the gospel." The verses are so simple: ● John 8:24, ● Luke 13:3, ● Matthew 10:32–33, ● Mark 16:16, and ● Revelations 2:10

The Passing of This Loved One is a Warning to All.

- We pass this way but once.
- Are we prepared for the journey of no return?

What Is Your Life?

A Funeral for an Aged Saint: James 4:14

Granville Brown

Occasions like this stir up deep emotions in our hearts. We are in the presence of two great mysteries—life and death.

Life is uncertain. Death is sure (1 Pet 1:24–25 Heb 9:27). "Death and decay and passing away have been written on the wings of time and timely things."

Our life at the most is short. The oldest person living would say that time has gone swiftly by. Since this is true, we should make the most of life—live a rich, full life. In considering this question, "What is your life?" we will study it under three headings:

I. WHAT IS THE ORIGIN OF LIFE?

- A. It is a gift of God (Gen 2:7).
- 1. God is the giver of every good and perfect gift (Jas 1:17)
- 2. God is the giver of life, and breath, and all things (Acts 17:25, 28)
- 3. God not only gives life, but also the things which sustain it (Matt 6:25–30)
- B . We should regard life as a gift from God, fall in love with life, and desire to live

- 1. God has taught us how to live so as to be happy and prosperous (1 Pet 3:10–12)
- 2. God has promised eternal life in the world to come (Luke 18:29–30)

II. WHAT IS THE MISSION OF LIFE?

- A. We should say with Paul: "For Me to Live is Christ, and To Die Is Gain" (Phil 1:21, Gal 2:20)
- 1. Can people see Christ in us? (Acts 4:13)
- 2. Christ came that we might have abundant life (John 10:10)
- 3. Christ showed us how to live (1 Pet 2:21, John 14:6)
- a. He lived a life of service (Mark 10:45)
- b. He went about "doing good" (Acts 10:38)
- c. He lived a life that has blessed the world, as Isaiah said in Isaiah 35:1–7.
- B. Our mission in life is well-illustrated by contrasting the life of Christ with the life of Methuselah
- 1. Christ lived on the earth for only 33 years, but the world has never been the same since. His influence still lives on today.
- 2. Genesis 5:27 All we know about Methuselah is recorded in one verse, though he was the oldest man who ever lived. He lived and he died. He left no influence for good. [It is thought that he died in the year of the Great Flood! Could that suggest anything about him?]

III. WHAT IS THE DESTINY OF LIFE?

- A. The desired destiny of life is to enjoy the rewards that come by reaping good things.

- 1. We believe the one who has departed lived a rich and full life in service of God. He tried to lose himself in the cause of Christ. Those who do that are promised eternal life (Matt 16:25).
- 2. Job described the blessings of a ripe old age as follows: "Thou shalt come to thy grave in a full age, like as a shock of corn cometh in his season" (Job 5:26). You see easily the anticipated joy of a rich, fruitful harvest at the end of life!
- B. As we near life's end, we take great comfort in the Scriptures.
- 1. Those who mourn our passing will be sincere and feel our influence in their own lives.
- 2. "Wherefore comfort one another with these words" (1 Thess 4:18; John 14:1–6; Ps 23, 116:15; Rev 14:13, 22:14).

Thoughts on the Death of a Youth

Wayne Emmons

Our purpose today is two-fold:

1. To pay our respects to the deceased
2. To endeavor to comfort the family

Death is a universal decree—No person can escape its sting. A natural question at a time such as this is: "Why did this happen?"

- Not one of us can really say, for no one knows except God.
- Notice the example of Abraham in Romans 4:18–22. Abraham did not know the "why," but he refused to dwell on that. He rather dedicated his life further to God as a life of service.

I. WHERE CAN WE FIND COMFORT IN THIS HOUR OF SORROW?

- A. We find comfort in memory
- God has given us a mind, a wonderful thing which will enable us to remember the good things. We

can remember the pleasant things about the deceased.
It is surely a great comfort to know that we have a
blessed memory of those gone on before.

- B. We find comfort in friends
-     The flowers, words of comfort and kindness,
and the many acts of friendship assure the family of a
great host of friends who are ever ready to rally to
their side in such a time of need.
- C. We find comfort in the Scriptures
-     1. Romans 15:4 All the inspired things written
earlier have been given to us that we "through the
patience and comfort of the Scriptures might have
hope."
-     2. Romans 8:28 Note: things "work together."
The passage does not affirm that everything that
happens to the Christian can be classified as good and
pleasant, but they "work together" with our
continuing faith to accomplish a good purpose.
-     3. Psalm 103:11–22
-     4. 1 Corinthians 10:13 When it seems that
something is too much to bear, remember this blessed
promise of the Lord. There is a way of escape [even if
it appears to come more slowly than we desire it] and
that is the way of faith.

II. WHAT POSSIBLE BENEFITS CAN COME FROM SUCH A TIME OF SORROW?

- A. We are assured of the host of friends that surround
us.
- B. It can serve to strengthen our faith. That sounds as
if it would not be a logical expectation, but it is so
often true that people feel closer to God when in
shattering burdens of life than when things are going
well. Notice the example of Job. He was patient in

tribulation and used adversity to strengthen his faith
(Job 1:20–22).

- C. It can cause us to ponder the uncertainty of life
  and make us aware that we should live soberly each
  day and be prepared at any time to meet our Maker
  (Jas 4:13–15).

To Heal the Broken-Hearted

Luke 4:18

John P. Murphree

Once again we find ourselves assembled with friends and neighbors to honor the memory of one of our citizens who has made his journey through the valley of the shadow of death.

- This is the journey from which none can escape (Heb 9:27).
- It almost always comes sooner than we realize (Jas 4:13–15).
- When it comes, those left behind are reminded that they have many friends (Rom 12:15, Gal 6:2).
- Let us think together about something suggested by Luke 4:18.
- Our purpose is not to set forth the life history of our friend who is gone, though there are many fine things which can be said about him.
- But we are dealing with those who are still here, those left behind, those who are "broken-hearted."

I. MANY THINGS CAN CAUSE PEOPLE TO BE BROKEN-HEARTED

A. Some are broken-hearted if they do not gain money and wealth.

    1. This should not be our goal in life (1 Tim 6:17).
    2. This is not the reason for broken hearts today.

B. Some are broken-hearted if they do not find fame and the applause of mankind.

    1. Neither should this be our goal (Ps 84:10).
    2. Such things as these are false ambitions that can cause broken hearts and keep one from doing God's will (2 Tim 6:9–10, John 12:41–42).

C. More often we are broken-hearted because of sickness, pain, death, and separation from those we love.

    1. Your hearts are broken today, not from loss of fame or fortune, but because you have lost one you love.
    2. Jesus is the great physician, and He is the only one I know who can heal broken hearts.

II. JESUS HAS GIVEN US A MESSAGE THAT SOOTHES BROKEN HEARTS

- A. It tells us that Jesus cares. We sing the song, "Jesus Cares."
- B. It says God loves us (Rom 5:8).
- C. It reminds us that we have something for which to live (Gal 2:20, Phil 3:13)
- D. It declares that our sorrows can soon be forgotten (Rom 8:18, 28).

Conclusion

Let us try harder each day to take advantage of our Great Physician who came to heal broken hearts. • Let us believe and obey Christ (Heb 5:8–9). • Let us spend more time in prayer (1 Pet 3:5). • Let us live closer to God. • The Song *"Guide Me, O Thou Great Jehovah,"* can mean much to us.

LOOKING FOR A CITY

HEBREWS 11:10, REVELATION 21:2–7

JOHN P. MURPHREE

- It is with a feeling of tenderness and love toward this family that we are assembled today to honor our brother and offer sympathy to them.
- It does not matter how familiar we are with death or how strong our faith in eternity; we are never quite ready to let a loved one go. We dread seeing them slip beyond that mysterious and dark curtain.
- This must be why God instructed Christians to "weep with those who weep." We can say that their sorrow does not have to be like those who have no hope.
- I believe our brother in Christ was looking for a City whose builder and maker is God.
- (Add obituary and other appropriate remarks about the deceased.)
- Abraham looked for the same city, and John also tells us something about it (Rev 21:4). Because our deceased friend was a Christian, a faithful Child of God, we can consider such Scriptures like this today with great comfort.

I. WHY IS THERE A LONGING IN OUR HEARTS TO LIVE IN THAT ETERNAL CITY?

- A. We long for it because we see how temporary and transient life is on earth
- •Ecclesiastes 1:4, • 2 Corinthians 4:18, •James 4:13–15, •Hebrews 13:14
- B. We long for it because the Bible tells us about a home of the soul
- •John 14:1–3, •John 5:28–29, •2 Corinthians 5:1, •Revelation 22:14
- We remember that Jesus had no earthly home (Matt 8:30). Was God better to the foxes and the birds? No! There was something better to come for Jesus—and there is something better to come for Christians!

II. THE BUILDER AND MAKER OF THAT CITY IS GOD

- A. That is why we turn to God's Word in times of sorrow for comfort
- •Romans 15:4, • 2 Corinthians 5:1
- B. That is why, today of all days, we cherish what God has said about salvation
- • Marks 16:15–16, •Acts 2:38, •Hebrews 5:8–9, • Revelation 2:10

III. WE AFFIRM OUR FAITH IN THAT CITY BECAUSE OF OUR CONVICTION ABOUT WHAT IS YET TO COME

- A. Why did our brother do what he did?
- • Why confess Christ? •Be baptized? •Attend worship faithfully? •Strive to live for Jesus? Because

he knew he would die—and he wanted to go to heaven! He was looking for a city!

- B. And so, when men like this man pass away, they leave us with hope!
- ●1 Thessalonians 4:13–18

Conclusion

We often sing "... I will cling to the old rugged cross, and exchange it some day for a crown." When we pass through that "dark and mysterious curtain" about which we know nothing, we exchange the iron shackles of this mortal body for the diamond ornament of immortality!

GONE

PSALM 90:1–10

CHARLES E. CROUCH

Some examples of the use of the term "gone" in the Bible:

- Job 7:14 "When I lie down, I say, 'When shall I arise, and the night be gone?' And I am full of tossings to and for unto the dawning of the day."
- 1 Kings 18:17, When Elijah taunted the false prophets about the failure of their god to respond to their pleas: "Cry aloud; for he is a god; either he is musing, or he is gone aside, or he is on a journey, or peradventure he sleepeth and must be awaked."

I. OUR FRIEND IS GONE. WHAT DOES IT MEAN?

- A. Song of Solomon 6:1 "Whither is thy beloved gone?"
- 1. His earthly life is gone (Ps 90:10)
- 2. There is always sadness at parting, but trials, tears, suffering, etc., are gone for the righteous dead (Rev 7:17, 14:13)
- B. His earthly opportunities are gone.
- 1. Time marches rapidly on (Jas 4:13–15)

- 2. Song of Solomon 2:11 "For, lo, the winter is past, the rain is over and gone."
- C. Gone but not forgotten.
- 1. His loved ones and friends will always remember him.
- 2. God also remembers (Heb 6:10)
- 3. Regarding Abel, it was said, "He being dead, yet speaketh" (Heb 6:10)
- D. Gone but not forever.
- 1. Death is not the end of life (Luke 16:19–31, Matt 22:32)
- 2. "For it is soon gone, and we fly away" (Ps 90:10)
- 3. He has gone to meet his Maker (Eccl 12:7)
- 4. He has gone to judgment and eternity
- 5. He has gone to join the righteous throng, awaiting judgment
- 6. We are thankful he went to Christ before he went to meet his Maker!
- E. We are all on a journey—a brief one!
- 1. We are just pilgrims here.
- 2. In view of this, there are some things we need to give special attention

II. MANKIND HAS GONE ON A LONG JOURNEY— INTO SIN AND DEATH

- A. Adam and Eve took a long journey—away from God! It was into "the far country" of sin (Gen 3).
- B. "There is a crying in the streets because of the wine; all joy is darkened, the mirth of the land is gone," (Isa 24:11)
- C. Some have "gone after other gods" (Jer 13:10)
- D. Sodom and Gomorrah had "gone after strange flesh" (Jude 7)

- E. "Many deceivers are gone forth into the world" (2 John 7)
- F. "All we like sheep have gone astray" (Isa 53:6, Ps 119:176)
- 1. "They are all gone aside" (Ps 14:3, 53:3)
- 2. "There is none righteous, no not one ... all have sinned ..." (Rom 3:10, 23)
- G. Because of this long journey taken for centuries by mankind, let us note

III. FOUR JOURNEYS OF CHRIST

- A. Jesus made the journey from heaven to earth
- 1. He came from God's throne to His footstool for 33 and 1/2 years
- a. Announced by prophets and by angels before and at birth
- b. From glory to suffering; from riches to poverty
- c. Still superior to Moses and Elijah
- 2. He journeyed from divine existence to human form
- a. Born of a virgin mother
- b. "Flesh" = the "form of a servant," in "likeness and fashion of a man"
- c. God spoke at His baptism and the Transfiguration to the "eyewitnesses of His majesty"
- 3. This journey was a dramatic demonstration of God's love for mankind.
- B. Jesus made the journey to the Cross
- 1. The new covenant was sealed with His blood (Matt 26:28, Heb 9:15)
- 2. We sing: "There Is A Fountain Filled With Blood"
- 3. His gospel now has great merit:

-         a. "Having been made perfect ..." (Heb 5:7–9)
-         b. He is "able to save to the uttermost" (Heb 7:25)
-         c. He is the "author and finisher of our faith" (Heb 12:2)
-     4. By this journey, the power of sin was defeated and destroyed.
- C. Jesus was gone from the empty tomb
-     1. "He is not here but is risen?" (Matt 28:6, John 20:11) What does this mean?
-     2. The power of death was conquered, and the fear of death was removed for Christians! (Rev 1:17–18, Heb 2:14–15, 2 Tim 1:10)
-     3. Our own resurrection is guaranteed (1 Cor 15:20–23)
-     4. The day of judgment is assured (Acts 17:31)
-     5. His gospel now has great power! (Rom 1:4, 16; Phil 3:10)
- D. Jesus has Gone to Heaven
-     1. "Having gone into heaven" (1 Pet 3:22)
-     2. "On the right hand of God" (Acts 2:33, Rom 8:34, Col 3:1)
-     3. "bring forth the royal diadem and crown Him Lord ..." (Ps 24:7–10, 1 Tim 3:16)
-     4. Luke 24:50–53, Acts 1:9–11
-     5. "One Lord," "head," etc. (Eph 4:5, Heb 1:3–4) "Oh, Worship the King ..."
-     6. His gospel now has love, merit, power, and hope of eternal glory!

IV. YOU AND I NEED TO JOURNEY BACK TO GOD THROUGH JESUS

- A. John 6:68 "Lord, to whom shall we go? ..."

- B. Our journey back to God out of the far country of sin has been made possible by the four journeys of Christ that He took.
- C. "Lo, the world is gone after Him .." (John 12:19) May it happen?
- D. "Your faith ... is gone forth ..." (1 Thess 1:8)

Conclusion

Have you gone to Christ?

The Christian life is just a brief journey here compared to eternity before we go to meet our Maker. Let us make sure we take this journey!

God's Arrangement for Burden-Bearing

Charles E. Crouch

Introduction:

- The pale horse and his rider have made another trip (Rev 6:8).
- This occasion reminds us that life has its duties, obligations, and burdens, which are common to man.
- This also reminds us that there are some things in life over which you and I as individuals have no control.
- It is fitting today that we study "God's arrangement for bearing burdens."

I. THERE ARE SOME BURDENS WE CAN HELP OTHERS TO BEAR (Gal 6:1,2)

- A. This is a service of love (Jas 5:19–20)
- B. The fulfillment of the law (Rom 13:10)
- C. We are "debtor" to our neighbor, and also our "brother's keeper" (Rom 1:14–15, Gen 4:9)
- D. We must trust others and depend upon them for things they can and should do for us.
- 1. We should never feel too independent of others
- 2. Over-confidence in self destroys

II. THERE ARE SOME BURDENS WE MUST BEAR OURSELVES (Gal 6:5)

- A. Occasions like this reveal burdens that individuals must bear themselves—we can be only sympathetic
- B. Each person is accountable to God (Rom 14:12)
- 1. There are many decisions in life each must make for himself
- 2. Each must mature and develop integrity personally
- 3. Obedience to Christ, including faithfulness in worship and service, is a personal responsibility of every man
- C. Some people assume to themselves responsibilities that others can, should, and must accept for themselves
- 1. It is not right to relieve children of either the decisions or the work they ought to assume to develop
- 2. This is also true of shirkers of duty
- D. We must have trust in ourselves and confidence in our own ability
- 1. Every person needs self-reliance
- 2. Lack of this in one's character leads to defeat

III. SOME BURDENS SHOULD BE CAST UPON THE LORD (1 Pet 5:6, 7)

- A. Cares and anxieties should be cast upon Him (Phil 4:6–7)
- B. There is much useless worry over things men cannot alter or control (Matt 6:31–32, Jas 4:14)
- C. Consider the attitude of David at the death of his child (2 Sam 12:23)

- D. Adam Clarke: "Anxiety cannot change the state or condition of anything from bad to good, but will infallibly injure your own souls."
- E. We must learn to trust in God and depend upon Him (Prov 3:5–6)

Three Kinds of Death

2 Corinthians 4:16–5:5

Charles E. Crouch

• Our brother has departed—a child of God has gone to meet his Maker.

• By God's grace, he lived long enough to create many precious memories that will live on in the hearts of family and friends—and in the mind of God.

• In view of the recent departure of our friend, may we now think of "Three Kinds of Death."

I. THERE IS DEATH *IN* SIN

- A. This is death "through your trespasses and sins ..." (Eph 2:1, 5)
- 1. Boy: "This my son was dead" (Luke 15:24, 32) This prodigal son was dead to righteousness, or right doing.
- 2. Woman: "She that giveth herself to pleasure is dead while she liveth," (1 Tim 5:6) Describes one dead to Christ and the love of God, who is in love with the world and its pleasures.
- 3. The church at Sardis: "... thou hast a name that thou livest and thou art dead" (Rev 3:1) "Be thou watchful, and establish the things that remain, which

were ready to die: for I have found no works of thine perfected before my God" (Rev 3:2).

- B. Death in sin is eternal separation from God (Isa 59:1–2) "Your iniquities have separated ..." (Rom 6:23) "The wages of sin is death ..."
- C. Death in sin is something to be feared greatly (Matt 10:28)

II. THERE IS DEATH *TO* SIN

- A. Christ "bare our sins in His body upon the tree, that we, having died to sins might live unto righteousness, by whose stripes ye were sealed" (1 Pet 2:24).
- B. "We who died to sin, how shall we any longer live therein?" (Rom 6:1–11)
-     1. "... buried with Him ... into death" (Rom 6:4)
-     2. "For if ... united with Him in likeness of His death ... also in the likeness of His resurrection ..." (Rom 6:5)
- C. Christ is God's power over death to sin: "Free gift of God is eternal life in Christ Jesus our Lord" (Rom 6:23) "As in Adam all die, so also in Christ shall all be made alive" (1 Cor 15:22) "The hour cometh, and now is, when the dead shall hear the voice of the Son of God; and they that hear shall live" (John 5:25). "And you did He make alive, when you were dead through your trespasses and sins ..." (Eph 2:1, 5, Col 2:13).
- D. "Death to sin" is cause for great joy (Acts 8:30, Acts 16:34)

III. THERE IS PHYSICAL DEATH ALSO—WHAT IS IT?

- A. Departure of the soul from the body, into the care and keeping of God (Gen 35:18, Eccl 12:7). "The body apart from the spirit is dead" (Jas 2:26). It is something common to all (Heb 9:27, John 14:1–2). It is something Jesus called "sleep" because of its temporary nature (John 11:11–14).
- B. Jesus abolished physical death by His resurrection (2 Tim 1:10; 1 Cor 15:20, 26; Heb.2:14–15; Rev 1:18). All who are in the tomb shall hear His voice and come forth (John 5:28–29).
- C. Psalm 116:15 "Precious in the sight of the Lord is the death of His saints."
- Revelation 14:13 "Blessed are the dead that die in the Lord."
- E. Philippians 1:23–24 It is better to depart and be with Christ. It is natural to want to stay with loved ones on earth, but we must accept God's will and the natural laws of life.
- F. Physical death is something that will be absent in heaven (Luke 20:36, Rev 21:4).

The God in Whom I Believe

Ephesians 4:6, Acts 17:22–31

Charles E. Crouch

When the dearest of earth is taken from us by the pale horse and his rider, our minds center upon God and the future life as never before. ● This was true of the noted unbeliever Robert Ingersoll who spoke at his brother's grave. ● All men want to know, "If a man die, shall he live again?" (Job 14:14). ● We will try to answer this question today by a study of "The God in Whom I Believe."

I. GOD IS ONE GOD, THE GOD OF ALL NATIONS— UNIVERSAL AND OMNIPRESENT

- A. Ephesians 4:6 "One God and Father of all who is over all, and through all and in all"
- 1. He is not just an American God, nor just a God of Israel
- 2. Acts 10:35 "In every nation ..."
- 3. Acts 17:26 "He made of one every nation of men ..."
- 4. Titus 2:13 "The great God ..."
- 5. 1 Timothy 1:17 "The only God ..."
- B. 1 Kings 20:23–30 He is "the God of the hills and the valleys ..."

- 1. Acts 17:27 "not far from each one of us", thus Omnipresent
- 2. Philippians 4:6 "at hand ..."
- C. He is the God of heaven and earth
- 1. Acts 17:24 "He being Lord of heaven and earth ..."
- 2. Matthew 6:9 "Our Father who art in heaven ..."
- 3. John 14:2 His is a house of "many rooms ..."
- 4. Matthew 6:26–29 Yet He is mindful of every sparrow and lily ...

II. HE IS A GOD OF UNLIMITED POWER— OMNIPOTENT

- A. He is the creator of heaven and earth
- 1. Acts 17:24 "The God that made the world and all ..."
- 2. Psalm 19:1 "The heavens declare ..." See also Genesis 1 and 2
- 3. The earth is; therefore, the earth's *Maker* is
- 4. Consider man's discoveries and achievements on earth: radio, TV, atomic energy, missiles, etc.—all of these simply are discoveries of the power and intelligence of the earth's *Maker*
- 5. Atheism assigns to the universe a totally inadequate *cause*. [Often, no cause at all, but rather only chance!]
- B. He is the creator of humans and the giver of life
- 1. Genesis 1:26, 2:7; Acts 17:25
- 2. Man is; therefore, man's *Maker* is
- 3. Consider man himself: his body and his ability to think and love. Love is a feeling of right, with a chemical foundation in the body. Where did this feeling come from? Chance? Did anyone ever see

love or thought? Weigh or measure them? These are just partial evidence of man's supernatural origin. Divinity must be his *Maker*!

-     4. Atheism assumes that life came from dead matter—a greater miracle than believing in the resurrection! (DeHoff).
- C. God is the sustainer of life and the universe through Christ (Heb 1:3, Col 1:16–17)

III. GOD IS THE FATHER OF CHRIST (Matt 17:5, Luke 1:31–33)

- A. He is the God of infinite love (1 John 4:8)
-     1. John 1:29 He gave Christ to redeem us from sin, see also John 3:16
-     2. 2 Corinthians 1:3 "the Father of mercies and God of all comfort"
-     3. 2 Peter 3:9 "Not willing that any should perish," therefore commands all men everywhere to repent (Acts 17:30–31)
- B. He is a God of grace, mercy, and also justice
-     1. Hebrews 12:6–11 Therefore, a God who chastises and scourges
-     2. Luke 12:4–5 Therefore, a God who "casts into hell"
- C. He is the God of the living, who raises the dead
-     1. Acts 2:24 "Whom God raised up, having loosed ...because it was not possible that He should be holden of it"
-     2. Acts 26:8 "Why is it judged incredible with you if God doth raise the dead?"
-     3. Compare to the caterpillar cocoon (Baxter's "*What Lies Beyond the Grave?*)
-     4. Matthew 22:29–32 "Ye do err, not knowing the Scriptures, nor the power of God ... not the God

of the dead, but of the living." See also Mark 12:24–26.

IV. HE IS THE GOD OF THE PAST, THE PRESENT, AND THE FUTURE—ETERNAL

- A. The God of the past
- 1. Exodus 3:6, Mark 12:26 "I am the God of Abraham, the God of Isaac, and the God of Jacob"
- 2. The God of Adam, Noah, Moses, Elijah, Peter, Paul, *et. al.*
- B. The God of the present
- 1. Psalm 46:1 "God is our refuge and strength, a very present help ..."
- 2. Psalm 23:4 "Yea, though I walk through the valley of the shadow of death ..."
- 3. 1 Peter 5:7 "He cares"—for every need See also Philippians 4:6–7, 19
- C. The God of the future—"Hope for Tomorrow"
- 1. Hebrews 13:8 "The same yesterday, and today, yea and forever"
- 2. Revelation 1:17–18 "Fear not; I am the first and the last, and the living one ..." See also Hebrews 2:14–15 and 2 Timothy 1:10
- 3. "He provides"—the giver of endless life
- 4. Campbell and Robert Owen debate: No fear, no hope—just like an ox!

V. HE IS THE GOD OF DIVINE REVELATION—THE GOD OF THE BIBLE

- A. A God of wisdom and knowledge—omniscient
- 1. Job 36:5, James 3:17, Ephesians 3:10, Ephesians 1:7–8, Psalm 104:24

- 2. 1 Samuel 2:3, Matthew 6:8, Acts 1:24, 1 Corinthians 3:19–20, 2 Timothy 2:19, Isaiah 55:7–9
- B. A God of revelation and reason
- 1. Deists think God has not spoken to man through the Bible
- 2. Man has not been left without guidance— God's will has been expressed (Matt 7:21, John 16:13, Eph. 5:17)
- 3. God's grace "instructs" (Titus 2:11–12; Acts 2:4, 38–41)
- 4. His gospel is reasonable (John 5:3, Rom 12:1, 1 Pet 3:15)
- C. A God in whom we can have faith—One we can trust and obey with a faith serene, abiding, and unshakable (2 Tim 1:12)
- 1. He is faithful and unchangeable (1 Cor 10:13, Jas 1:17)
- 2. He is a perpetual source of strength and power.
- D. A God to be feared with reverence and awe (Heb 12:28–29, Titus 2:11–14)

ONE STEP BETWEEN
RALPH BURRIS

I. BACKGROUND TO THIS TEXT

Again, we are made to realize that our journey is but for a little while.

On one occasion, David expressed the nearness of death to him (1 Sam 20:3).

It would help us also to ponder James 4:14

II. SOME CHARACTERISTICS ABOUT THE "STEP OF DEATH"

- A. It is a certain step (Heb 9:27)
- 1. Nothing is more certain than death (Job 14:1–2, 1 Cor 15:22, 1 Pet 1:24)
- 2. Reminders are constantly before us: •Every cemetery we see •When we feel pain, suffering, weariness • We are in each funeral procession somewhere.
- B. Yet, it is also an uncertain step
- 1. Nothing is more uncertain than the "how" and the "when" it will come to us
- 2. David realized there was "but a step" between life and death

- 3. Genesis 27:2 [Isaac said to Esau: "I am old. I do not know the day of my death." He thought that a final gesture of kindness would be a blessing.]
- C. It is a parting step
- 1. In death, there is a separation of the soul and the body. The body returns to the earth and the spirit returns to God (Eccl 12:7).
- 2. The soul awaits the judgment (Heb 9:27).
- 3. All earthly relationships are terminated; the plans of the deceased are gone. Earthly ties and toil cease. See Ecclesiastes 9:5–6.
- 4. 1 Timothy 6:7 One leaves the world of nature, earthly possessions, and tender ties.
- D. It is a solitary step
- 1. We do not know what it is like in that we have no first-hand information and the dead do not return to tell us about it.
- 2. Psalm 23:4 Though death is our most lonely experience, God's people do not fear it: "Though I walk through the valley of the shadow of death, I will fear no evil, for Thou art with me!"
- E. It is a solemn step
- 1. In life, we often refuse to face realities that are unpleasant. Then, we will be brought "face to face" with things we might like to hide. See Revelation 6:15–17; Luke 23:29–30
- 2. Bible teaches we need to face (Heb 9:27, Luke 12:20, Rev 14:13).

Conclusion:

Jesus Christ has made it possible that this step might be a rich one for us (2 Cor 8:9).

May we always seek the peace of mind and soul which comes from the Word of God.

WHAT IS LIFE?

RALPH BURRIS

I. THE MINDSET SUCH AN OCCASION PRESENTS
TO US

On occasions like this, we are made to realize that this world is
not our home and that we have here no continuing city. Those
thoughts should prompt us to search our hearts about where our
greater emphases in life are (1 Pet 1:24, Jas 4:1).

II. WHAT IS LIFE? SOME THINGS WE MUST
CONCLUDE ABOUT IT

- A. Life is created by God
- 1. God created humans in His own image and
placed them above the rest of creation (Gen 1:26–27,
Ps 8:3–9).
- 2. The body is from the dust, and the spirit
came from God (Gen 2:7, Eccl 12:7).
- 3. At death, this union is dissolved (Eccl 12:7,
Jas 2:26).
- B. The life is more than "meat"
- 1. Jesus taught this principle in Luke 12:23,
"The life is more than food, and the body is more
than clothing."

- 2. Jesus also taught this when He was tempted (Matt 4:4).
- 3. That is why the soul must be fed on the eternal word of God (Ps 119:97; Eccl 12:13; John 6:27, 32–33, 51).
- C. Life requires trust in God
- 1. Jesus also taught this principle (Matt 6:25)
- 2. Paul expressed this trust (2 Cor 5:6–9)
- D. Life Needs Guidance
- 1. David understood this truth (Ps 16:11). "You will show me the path of life; in Your presence is fullness of joy. At Your right hand are pleasures forevermore."
- 2. The need for guidance is also expressed in Psalm 119:47–48, 105. "Thy Word is a lamp/light to my path."
- 3. It is in the Word of God that the hope of man is revealed (Ps 119:81).
- 4. Think: It is only in God's Word, the eternal truth, that we are told from whence we came, why we are here, and what lies beyond the grave for us.
- E. Life gives us fullness and richness, but only if hidden in service to God
- 1. What is meant by this? It means that one has submitted self totally to God by being His child and following Christ (Col 3:1–3). "If ... you are raised with Christ, seek those things which are above, where Christ is, sitting at the right hand of God. Set your mind on things above, not on things on the earth. For you died, and your life is hidden with Christ in God."
- 2. All of our activities are directed toward heaven and the result for the faithful Christian is to be with God and Christ in glory (Col 3:4). "When Christ who is our life appears, then you also will appear with Him in glory."

Conclusion:

We are convinced that these thoughts were the faith of the deceased we honor today. These are also the thoughts we all need to live by. If we do so, then we may make our calling and election sure and have hope for an abundant entrance into heaven (2 Pet 1:10–11).

The Certainty of Death

Ralph Burris

We have come together because of the call of death—an event that is constantly occurring around us within our own families and acquaintances. Death is a silent preacher, teaching us that this world is not our abiding place. It reminds us that we are in the land of the dying, rapidly nearing the end of life. We need to contemplate seriously how we are prepared for the future.

I. DEATH PROMPTS A QUESTION: "WHAT IS IMPLIED IN DYING?"

- A. The question cannot be fully answered because we have no first-hand information.
- 1. No one living has experienced it and returned to give us information.
- 2. The Bible gives us all the light which we have regarding it.
- B. Death is a separation of the soul from the body.
- 1. God made us as compound beings, composed of body and soul (Gen 2:7).
- 2. At death, this union is dissolved (Eccl 12:7).
- C. Death is a departure from this world, for "here we have no continuing city."

-      1. The unprepared person has fear and dread in his heart as he approaches death.
-      2. The child of God can view death as a release from this life and the beginning of one that is far better (Rev 21:4, Phil 1:21).
- D. Death is an entrance upon a new state of existence, as the soul goes into the spirit realm.

II. THE LIFE AND DEATH OF THIS ONE IS A SOLEMN TESTIMONY THAT WE ARE FACING THE SAME EXPERIENCE

- A. After any one is born, there is the inevitable appointment with God (Heb 9:27).
- B. The Bible pictures life as being very brief (1 Pet 1:24, Jas 4:14).
-      1. Each moment, somewhere someone is passing into eternity.
-      2. We cannot escape the conclusion that someday we must die.
- C. As time passes, every pain we feel and every degree of suffering is a reminder that we will not live forever.

III. BECAUSE DEATH IS CERTAIN, WE ASK, "WHAT CAN WE DO?"

- A. The life of Jesus was brief, yet He made His life rich, full, and deep by contributing much to the welfare of mankind. He was known for going "about doing good" (Acts 10:38).
- B. We should strive to improve the various scenes of life through which we pass, to leave the world a better place because we have lived in it.
- C. Specifically, to be prepared for our death

experience, we should seek that spiritual life that cannot be destroyed by death.

- 1. God has given us the Bible, the book of instructions, as our guidebook. It tells us about the new birth and how to become Christians so we can "die in the Lord."

- 2. The one who is spiritually alive may then look at death without fear. He has nothing to fear, but everything to hope for. (1 Thess 4:13–18, 1 Cor 15:50–57).

Conclusion

Our goal: Always remember that life is brief, death is certain, and eternity is long. Our primary interest while here should always be to seek the spiritual life in Christ Jesus, the life that death cannot destroy.

Suffer Them to Come

Matthew 19:14

Ralph Burris

Read Matthew 18:1–6.

From this reading, we can learn some things that will provide comfort for us on this sad occasion.

I. WE LEARN THAT JESUS LOVED THE LITTLE ONES

- A. Although Jesus was busy, He had time to show love to little children. He used them to teach a great lesson about the nature of His Kingdom.
- B. He rebuked His disciples for their indifference (Matt 18:6, Matt 19:14)
- C. The death of a child, including an infant, is always sad.
- D. The death of a little one is always difficult to understand.

II. WE LEARN THERE IS A BRIGHT SIDE, EVEN IN THE MIDST OF SADNESS

- A. We know that God loves our children even more than we do, and we can find comfort by knowing they are in His presence. They go to be with Christ in heaven because they do not come into this world inheriting any guilt. They are spiritually innocent and safe (Ezek 18:20).

- B. They are spared the cares and sorrows of life (Mark 10:14–15).
- C. They never taste the pangs of personal sin (Matt 18:10, 14).
- D. Their salvation is forever secure (Matt 18:10).
- E. David understood this (2 Sam 12:23). We should learn like David to be spurred to live in such a way that we can go to be with them.
- F. This poem may mean something to us as words of comfort:

Go to thy rest fair child;
Go to thy dreamless bed.
While yet so gentle, undefiled,
With blessings on thy head.

Before thy heart had learned
In waywardness to stray;
Before thy feet had ever turned
The dark and downward way.

Ere sin had seared the breast,
Or sorrow woke the tear,
Rise to thy home of changeless rest
In your celestial sphere.

Shall love, with weak embrace,
Thy upward wing detain?
No! Gentle angel, seek thy place
Amid the cherub train.

Blessed Are the Dead

Revelation 14:13

Claud Lamar, Jr.

I. "BLESSED ARE THE DEAD ..."

- A. The condition of those who die in the manner which is immediately specified is to be regarded as a blessed, or happy one.
- B. There is so much in death that is sad; we so much dread it by nature. It cuts us off from so much that is dear to us, and the grave is so cold and cheerless as a resting place.
- C. We owe so much, therefore, to God for a system of grace that enables us to say and feel that blessedness or happiness can be found in death.

II. "... WHO DIE IN THE LORD ..."

- A. This phrase applies the above promise to those who are followers of Christ, Christians. It applies to those who have been reconciled to God in the body of Christ.
- B. How does one come into this relationship?

- 1. Earlier, man has separated himself from God by sin.
- 2. Then one can be reconciled through Christ and the Word (2 Cor 5:17–19, Rom 1:16).
- 3. The gospel teaches one to ●Believe in Jesus as God's Son ●Repent of all sins ●Confess Christ as God's Son and ●Be baptized into Christ (Gal 3:27, Rom 6:3–4)
- C. This phrase could not, of course, apply to one who has refused to obey the Lord and to live in harmony with His teaching in the New Testament.

III. "... THAT THEY MAY REST FROM THEIR LABORS ..."

- A. "Labors"—literally "wailing" and "grief," but also denotes toil, labor, effort.
- B. The term is used here in the sense of wearisome toil, hardships, and grief encountered by the servant of God as he strives to live and serve God and his fellow man.
- C. Life is not always easy. The Christian life is not always doing the easiest things. There is much to do; hardships often come, and grief is sometimes ours but to those who continue steadfastly, God promises rest.
- D. This thought is further developed by John in Revelations 21:4.

IV. "... FOR THEIR WORKS FOLLOW THEM."

- A. Reward for their work and service will be with them.
- B. Thus Paul told the Corinthians (1 Cor 15:58, 2 Cor 5:10).

- C. This is all that can follow a man into eternity (Matt 6:19–20).

Conclusion:

Thus, we have the great promise of Christianity: "Blessed are the dead who die in the Lord from henceforth; yea, saith the Spirit, that they may rest from their labors; for their works follow them" (Rev 14:13).

GOD'S PLANS THAT COMFORT IN DEATH

REVELATION 14:13

CLAUD LAMAR, JR.

We are gathered to pay respect as friends and loved ones to one who has left us.

Death is a separation of the spirit and the body.

It is not ours to judge but rather to think together about things that would be best for all of us concerned.

I. BIBLE TRUTHS CONCERNING LIFE

- A. We are here but for a little while (Ps 103:13–16, Jas 4:14, Luke 12:15–21
- B. Death is universal (Heb 9:27, 1 Cor 15:51–53)
- C. Judgment is promised (Matt 25, 2 Cor 5:10, Rom 14:10–12, Rev 20:11–21:4).
- D. Our eternal destiny (Matt 25).

II. GOD'S PLAN FOR OUR SALVATION

- A. It is impossible for us to save ourselves (Jer 10:23, Rom 3:23, 1 John 1:8).
- B. God's grace abounds through Jesus Christ (Eph 1:7, 5:21). Planned from the beginning.

- C. God planned for salvation so that by the preaching of the Gospel (Rom 1:16), men might learn about Christ and come to Him (1 Pet 1:9–12).
- D. Thus Jesus sent the Apostles forth with the Great Commission that all might be prepared for the hour of death (Mark 16:15–16, Acts 2:38).
- E. If we meet death unprepared, it will not be because God has not loved us and provided a way for us.

III. THE JOY OF THOSE WHO PREPARE

- A. Paul taught us about it (1 Thess 4:13–18)
- B. Paul felt personal joy in what he looked forward to (2 Tim 4:7–8)
- C. John's picture of heaven has comforted all of us (Rev 21).

A FUNERAL FOR A
CHRISTIAN WOMAN
JOE D. GRAY

Every cradle asks the question, "From whence did we come?"
Every grave ponders the serious query: "Where do we go?"
Man has tried vainly from his own wisdom to answer both of these questions for thousands of years. Every attempt to deny God as the Creator and Destiny of all creation has but ended in hopeless confusion or in foolish worship of material things. Only God can answer these questions properly! (Prayer)

I. FROM WHERE DID I COME?

- A. God says, "In the beginning God created ..." What is the source of the life that has now departed? The source is an all-powerful, all-wise, everlasting, constant-loving God.
- B. The human body and the human mind are powerful forces—the most powerful among material things. They can accomplish great things.
- Though humans are made to walk, they can fly. They can sail a thousand times farther than they can swim.
- They can send rockets hundreds of thousands of miles into the air. They can send messages, even pictures, through space. They can discover medicines

to conquer dreaded diseases, lengthening life by many years.

II. WHAT THEN IS THE DESTINY OF THIS GREAT BEING?

- A. Man says death is our destiny.
- B. God says we must die—indeed, that it is best that we die.
- Psalm 90:10 To live longer is pain (escapes pain).
- Revelation 14:13 "Blessed are the dead that die in the Lord" (finds joy)
- Psalm 116:15 "Precious in the sight of the Lord is the death of His saints…"
- It brings joy to God: My child is coming home (if a saint)
- A life of rebellion is closed (if an unforgiven sinner)
- C. Thus, every person has an appointment with death, but death is not our final destiny.
- D. Hebrews 9:27 "After death … the judgment …"
- 2 Corinthians 5:10 The spiritual and moral quality of our lives determines the nature of our destiny—good or bad.
- Thus, death is not the end, but a separation (2 Cor 5:6–9) willing to be absent …
- E. The fullness of life then is to be ready for our destiny.

III. THERE ARE MANY NOTES OF JOY ON THIS OCCASION OF SORROW

- A. There is the memory of her devotion to her family and her family's devotion to her.

- B. There is the love she had for her friends and their love for her.
- C. There was her smile ... found often even as death approached.
- D. But more ... there was her love for eternity and for God!
- She prepared for death, having by faith been baptized into Christ
- She loved the church and wanted very much to return to regular attendance
- She loved me, not because I deserved it, but because I preached the gospel
- She set an example for her family and friends
- She was constant in prayers. They prepare and cause true respect for her today.

Conclusion
1 Thessalonians 4:13–18
(Closing remarks appropriate for the occasion.)

A Funeral for a Christian Youth

Joe D. Gray

Scriptures: 1 Corinthians 2:9, John 14:1–3, 2 Corinthians 1:3–4
(Opening remarks, Obituary, Prayer)
I. WHEREVER YOUTH IS FOUND, LOVE IS FOUND

- A. Christ demonstrated His love for young people (Matt 18).
- B. Today, it is utterly impossible for me to express in words the pain that lives in my heart. Death of a youth is more painful than that of a mature person. Illust.: A doctor once told me, "I never get used to death, but of all deaths, that of the young hurts most."
- C. Some characteristics of most youth: ●A smile ●Cooperation ●Kindness to all ●Faithfulness toward the church ●A longing to be loved and respected (especially by family).

II. SOME GREAT LESSONS THAT WE MUST REMEMBER TODAY

- A. The great need for parental training and the tragedy if it is neglected.

- 1. This is a happy instance in which that lesson has been illustrated. The father and mother trained their son. They taught him, loved him, and have no reason to regret their efforts.
- 2. But consider how much more sad it would be had they neglected that.
- B. The necessity of obedience to God, even in youth
- 1. Hebrews 9:27 "... it is appointed unto men once to die, but after this the judgment."
- 2. Their son obeyed at an early age and I shall never forget having the opportunity to assist him in his obedience. Many people wait too long to obey the gospel.
- C. Even in youth, we must recognize the proper values of life and prepare for the next life
- 1. Parents, please cultivate in your child(ren) a love for the Lord.
- 2. Young people, never deny the greatness of those who have given you so much.
- 3. Remember God, especially Ecclesiastes 12:1 "Remember now thy Creator in the days of thy youth..."
- 4. 1 Timothy 4:9–12 "Let no man despise thy youth; but be thou an example ..."

III. A STORY FOR THE PARENTS

- A. 2 Samuel 12:15b–23 When David's child died, he said: "But now he is dead, wherefore should I fast? Can I bring him back again? I shall go to him, but he shall not return to me ..."
- B. (Closing remarks as appropriate.)

A Funeral for a Christian Man

Joe D. Gray

I. SUMMARIZE THE STORY OF THE BIRTH AND DEATH OF CHRIST

- A. Scriptures ●Matthew 1:20–21, ●Luke 2:7–14, ●Matthew 27:33–35a, ●Matthew 27:45–46, ●Matthew 27:50–54, ●1 Corinthians 15:19–22, ●1 Corinthians 15:25–26
- B. Prayer

II. FROM CHILDHOOD, WE ASK "WHY" ABOUT MANY THINGS

- A. We ask about the Painful and Unpleasant Things of Life
- 1. God has supplied many answers in the Bible. Some He has not (Deut 29:29).
- 2. Many things God cannot explain to us because we are utterly incapable of understanding.
- B. Imagine how many times Jesus might have asked, "Why?"
- 1. Why Nazareth rejected Him.

- 2. Why those He healed were so ungrateful (Luke 10:17)
- 3. On the Cross: "My God, My God, why hast thou....?"(Matt 27:46)

III. WE SHOULD USE ADVERSITY

- A. It is difficult to understand Christ's death
- 1. By His death, mankind can be saved.
- 2. He used it and so does God.
- B. All forms of adversity, when rightly borne, may be used ... as stepping stones to victory rather than stumbling stones to defeat.
- 1. Adversity teaches others to rely on God.
- 2. It teaches others to pray.
- 3. It increases our ability to sympathize:

> *For every hill I've had to climb,*
> *For every stone that bruised my feet,*
> *For all the blood and sweat and grime,*
> *For blinding storms and burning heat,*
> *My heart sings but a grateful song—*
> *These were the things that made me strong!*
> *For all the heartaches and the tears,*
> *For all the anguish and the pain,*
> *For gloomy days and fruitless years,*
> *And for the hopes that lived in vain,*
> *I do give thanks, for now I know*
> *These were the things that helped me grow!*

- C. The story of Christ, though a story of death, is a story of hope.
- 1. He left heaven for us on earth.
- 2. He lived.

-      3. He suffered and died ... that we might live. The darkest hour was right after death.

IV. SUFFERING HERE IS NOT TO BE COMPARED WITH GLORY OVER THERE (Rom 8:18, 20, 22)

- A. John 14:18–21 "... I will come to you ..."
-      1. Into the sick room.
-      2. Into the operating room.
-      3. Into the lonely abode of old age.
-      4. Even into the room of death ... HE COMES.
- B. He comes to bring hope ...
-      1. To the faithful "Sorrow not, even as others which have no hope ..." (1 Thess 4:13).
-      2. The unfaithful do not have hope. • The celebrated unbeliever Robert Ingersoll: "Whether in mid-sea or among the breakers of the farther shore, a wreck at last must mark the end of each and all. And every life, no matter if its every hour is rich with love, and ever moment jeweled with a joy, will, at its close, become a tragedy as sad and deep and dark as can be woven out of the warp and woof of the mystery of death. ... Life is a narrow veil between the cold and barren peaks of two eternities. We strive in vain to look beyond its heights. We cry aloud, and the only answer is the echo of our wailing cry."
- C. Our departed Christian brother knew the hope that Ingersoll denied. He saw a glory that Ingersoll refused. He heard an answer that entered not into the soul of the great atheist.

V. TO THOSE LEFT BEHIND, LET US SET A GOAL AND WORK TOWARD IT.

(Remarks as appropriate to close the service.)

Divine Assistance in Time of Sorrow

Joe D. Gray

Scripture Readings: ● 2 Corinthians 1:3–4, ● 1 Corinthians 15:19–26, ● 2 Corinthians 5:10, ●Psalm 116:1–4

Burdens of sorrow often seem heavier than we can bear and heavier than we can lift. Yet we have cause to notice with gratitude the many aids offered to us by our Heavenly Father.

I. LIFE IS COMPOSED OF MANY EMOTIONS

- The emotional capacity of man is very complex. Our emotions range from ecstasy to despair. There are many degrees in between so that no one emotion ever holds complete sway.
- In moments of ecstasy, our hearts do not burst because we have knowledge that someday, we shall have cause to cry again.
- In moments of deepest bereavement, our hearts refrain from breaking because we can view, faintly in the distance, the light of a smile once more. Such acknowledgment, even upon an occasion of death, is not irreverent. It is but a recognition of the design of God to assist us in a curse-weary world.

- God uses the power of memory and the force of forgetfulness to buoy us in the midst of pain. Therefore, the memory of this loved one will find a way to bring joy to our hearts through gratitude for having known and loved him. On the other hand, the force of forgetfulness will ease the pain of this moment and help bring smiles to our hearts again.

II. THE IMPACT OF THE LOVE OF FRIENDS

- The love of our friends is another force God immobilizes to assist us in times of sorrow. As we view the way God loves us, we learn that love for others is an unending source of strength and joy. In times like this, therefore, we find strength and courage in the concern and sympathy shown to us by our many friends.
- In the past hours, doubtlessly, this great force has been of assistance to you. The emotional strength derived from the impact of the love of our friends helps us in many ways to counteract the feeling of helplessness, gloom, and despair of this moment.

III. A KNOWLEDGE OF VICTORY IN DEATH

- It is acknowledged by practically all humans that death, as the wage of sin, is humanity's greatest enemy. God adds His word of endorsement to the truthfulness of that assumption: "The last enemy ... is death."
- While acknowledging this fact, God assures us that all of our enemies can be conquered—even the enemy, death (1 Cor 15:19–22, 25–26).
- Death, in reality, is merely a step from one existence to another. More correctly, it is the step from one phase

of existence to another phase of the same existence because we will always have the same identity.

- Death is a passing away, not from existence as a whole, but from earthly existence through a gate, into a valley that previously was veiled from our view.
- Death is also referred to as a rest or a sleep. It is a separation from an old existence and old acquaintances to a state of awaiting the final judgment.
- Since death is a separation, it is always accompanied by sorrow. We never enjoy being separated from those we love. Nothing said or done can completely remove that sorrow—not even our mixture of emotions, the power of memory, the force of forgetfulness, or the impact of the love of our friends.
- Our friend and loved one then has departed this life and is in the care and keeping of God, awaiting that last day. His destiny is in the hand of the Creator, and it is to God that we commend his spirit (1 Cor 4:3–5).

IV. FROM THIS EXPERIENCE, WE LEARN:

- "It is appointed man to die." Seeing more clearly now the certainty of death, we should resolve today to make things ready while yet there is time.
- The message of the Bible to those who are still alive on earth when loved ones have preceded them in death is always a message of action. God spoke to Joshua and told him: "Moses, My servant, is dead." Then He added: "Now, therefore, arise and go into the land I promised thee." (Josh 1:2, 7–9).
- When the Apostles were troubled over the impending departure of Jesus to heaven, Christ gave them the Great Commission, and His message was: "Go ye into all the world, and preach the gospel to every creature."

To those of us here bereaving the loss of a loved one or friend, we should remember that Jesus Christ is the "author of eternal salvation unto all them that obey Him" (Heb 5:9). And thus, "Be thou faithful unto death" that we might receive the crown of life (Rev 2:10).

- This is the plea of God; it is the plea of the Spirit; it is the plea of Christ (the Word). Such would be the plea of our loved one: could he speak to us today. Such, indeed, is the plea of death as a whole.

A Funeral for an Elder in the Church

Joe D. Gray

I. MAN'S PROBLEM: SUCCESS

- A. History has been portrayed as a vain search for success (plan, work, fight, fail).
- B. The baffling part of the struggle is the brief nature of life.
- 1. Death always faces us.
- 2. The highest and brightest tomorrows are snatched away.
- C. Without God, futures are always black.
- 1. Ingersoll, the celebrated unbeliever: "Life is a narrow vale between the cold and barren peaks of two eternities. We strive in vain to look beyond the heights. We cry aloud, and the only answer is the echo of our wailing cry. From the voiceless lips of the unreplying dead, there comes no word."
- 2. Ingersoll, continuing: "For, whether in mid sea or among the breakers of the farther shore, a wreck must mark at last the end of each and all. And every life, no matter if its every hour is rich with love and every moment jeweled with a joy, will, at its close,

become a tragedy, as sad and deep, and dark as can be woven of the warp and woof of mystery and death."

- D. The Poet has asked:

> *Is it true, O Christ in Heaven,*
> *That whichever way we go,*
> *Walls of darkness must surround us,*
> *Things we would but cannot know?*
> *That the infinite must bound us*
> *Like a temple veil unrent,*
> *Whilst the finite ever wearies,*
> *So that none's therein content?*

II. THE VOICE FROM DEATH (OVERLOOKED BY INGERSOLL)

- A. The empty tomb of Joseph speaks: "But now is Christ risen from the dead, and become the firstfruits of them that slept. For since by man came death, by man came also the resurrection of the dead. For as in Adam all die, even so in Christ shall all be made alive" (1 Cor 15:20–22).
- 1. "…Why seek ye the living among the dead?" (Luke 24:5)
- 2. "… He is not here, for He is risen, as He said …" (Matt 28:6).
- B. Matthew 11:28–30 "Come unto me, all ye that labour and are heavy laden, and I will give you rest. Take My yoke upon you, and learn of Me; for I am meek and lowly in heart, and ye shall find rest unto your souls. For My yoke is easy, and My burden is light."
- C. Hebrews 5:8–9: "Though He were a Son, yet learned He obedience by the things which He suffered; and being made perfect, He became the

author of eternal salvation unto all them that obey
Him."

III. HEEDING THIS VOICE BRINGS SUCCESS OUT OF MATERIAL FAILURE. MATERIAL SUCCESS IS NAUGHT WITHOUT THIS VOICE.

- A. (Our deceased friend and brother) listened; he believed; he followed.
- 1. His life looked forward to success, never backward.
- 2. His life was Christ-centered.
- B. I am not here to predict his destiny.
- 1. I am too weak and frail to have even a voice in such.
- 2. But, gladly, I rest his care with our God, believing that "to live is Christ; to die is gain."
- 3. Death is always: sudden, regardless of the tardiness of approach •Surprising, regardless of preparation. •Sorrowful, regardless of the state of the soul.
- 4. Yet, the sorrow is directed toward us, not to him: "Precious in the sight of the Lord is the death of His saints" (Ps 116:15).

IV. (OUR CHRISTIAN FRIEND) WAS NOT ONLY A CHRISTIAN, BUT HE WAS A CHRISTIAN SELECTED BY FELLOW SAINTS TO SERVE IN GOD'S HIGHEST OFFICE IN THIS LIFE.

- A. The New Testament church is organized with a provision for elders (Phil 1:1).
- B. The qualifications of elders are given (1 Tim 3:2–7).
- 1. Duties are given for elders:

-        ●Acts 20:28 "Take heed therefore unto yourselves, and to all the flock, over the which the Holy Ghost hath made you overseers, to feed the church of God, which He hath purchased with His own blood."
-        ●Hebrews 13:17 "Obey them that have the rule over you, and submit yourselves; for they watch for your souls, as they that must give account, that they may do it with joy, and not with grief, for that is unprofitable for you."
-        2. Duties are given for members:
-        ●As stated in Hebrews 13:17, members are to obey them in all that is right.
-        ●2 Timothy 5:17 "Let the elders that rule well be counted worthy of double honor, especially they who labour in the word and doctrine."
- C. The witness of this congregation is that he did a difficult job well!

Conclusion:

Who is a Faithful Elder?

He is a man of God on earth who sacrifices all,
And lives in princely poverty to heed the church's
    call.

He ministers to all the needs of both the rich and
    poor,
And guides them in the struggle and strife they
    must endure.

He teaches them to think of God instead of worldly
    gain,

And why the sun must share the sky with clouds
    that carry rain.

He undertakes to aid the sick, to help the blind
    to see,
And show the lame the way to walk in love and
    sympathy.

And when he does his duty well, he sanctifies
    the sod,
And by his good example, proves he was a man
    of God.

MYSTERIES

JESS M. WILCOXSON

Life, as well as death, is a mystery. The brevity of life is affirmed (Job 14:1, Ps 9:6, 10, Jas 4:14).

I. THE CERTAINTY OF DEATH

- A. Ecclesiastes 8:8, 9:5; Hebrews 9:27
- B. Our experiences teach us: All that tread the globe know that a few more days will only bring death.

II. THEN WHAT?

- A. Then the Judgment will follow (Heb 9:27)
- B. Is Death a Blessing or a Curse?

1. Death is universal and unconditional
2. Resurrection is universal and unconditional
3. Salvation is offered universally but is conditional

- C. Death is a Blessing to a Child of God.

1. Ecclesiastes 7:1
2. Philippians 1:21

   3. Revelation 14:13
   4. John 14:1–6
   5. "Precious in the eyes of the Lord ..."
   6. 2 Corinthians 5:1–10
   7. 1 Thessalonians 4:13–19

- D. Death is the gateway to joy or to sorrow: It all depends on how we live, not how we die.

III. DISCUSS 1 CORINTHIANS 15: "The Sting of Death"
All the mysteries will fade when before God we stand and are found just in His sight.
Psalm 139:7–9

THE PROBLEM OF LIFE
JESS M. WILCOXSON

What is Life? What is the best way to live? These are questions that interest all of all ages, including the pagan or atheist, the infidel, or Christian

The Solution? Christ's mission, life, and death. Let us consider.

I. WHAT IS THE CHRIST LIFE? WHAT IS A CHRISTIAN LIFE?

- A. To know God (John 17:3)
- B. To be a child of God.

II. IT IS THE LIFE THAT WE ARE CREATED TO LIVE

- A. Ecclesiastes 12:13–14, Micah 6:8
- B. All others are missing the mark, the mission—and end in failure.
- C. Success comes as we live as Christ would have us live.

III. IT IS THE ONLY LIFE THAT HONORS GOD

- A. John 14:6–7
- B. This life honors the wisdom of God and anything else defies and rejects it.

IV. IT IS THE LIFE THAT DEVELOPS THE RIGHT KIND OF LIFE

- A. All duties are enjoined and discharged in this life only (Titus 2:11–12)
- B. No other life will make us like Christ (Col 3:10).

V. IT IS THE ONLY LIFE THAT HAS REAL PROMISES CONNECTED

Ephesians 2:12–22: It is the only life that ensures eternal happiness

Thy Will Be Done

Jess M. Wilcoxson

When the Lord came face to face with death, it was His desire to escape it, but His prayer was, "Not My will, but Thine be done." Let us consider:

I. GOD'S WILL IN THE AFFAIRS OF THIS LIFE

- A. The sun to shine on the just and the unjust (Matt 5:45)
- B. One event unto all (Eccl 9:2)

II. GOD'S WILL IN OUR SALVATION

- A. Belief and obedience (Acts 10:43, Rom 6:17)
- B. Man cannot improve upon it (Gal 1:8)

III. GOD'S WILL IN DEATH

- A. An appointment we must keep (Heb 9:27)
- B. The deaths of loved ones often bring us to ●God, as we depend on our dependence upon Him ●to friends, as we appreciate their presence and words of encouragement, and ●to ourselves, as we are made

aware of our need for self-examination and
preparation for this event in our lives.

IV. GOD'S WILL IN JUDGMENT

- A. All will be judged (Heb 9:27)
- B. The standard of judgment (Acts 17:31, Rom 2:16)
- C. Preparation for that day (2 Pet 3:11–12)

Conclusion:

The Savior is our great example and our perfect pattern for life. When He entered the Garden of Gethsemane, He prayed, "Not My will but Thine be done." May our prayer be His prayer, and may our attitude be His attitude when the sorrow of death comes.

DEATH

2 CORINTHIANS 4:18, 5:10, 1 CORINTHIANS 15

JESS M. WILCOXSON

I. DEATH IS ALWAYS AN UNPLEASANT GUEST

- A. It never fits our plans. It gives no consideration for ●Timing ●Circumstances ●Conditions
- B. As no respecter of persons, it comes to ●Young and Old ● Busy and Idle ● Rich or Poor.

II. DEATH IS UNIVERSAL AND UNCONDITIONAL

- A. Ecclesiastes 9:5
- B. Is no escape. It is a power we cannot overcome ● Can only be delayed at times by science

III. DOES DEATH "END IT ALL?"

- A. Job 14:14
- B. If so, life has no meaning. "Before we learn to live, we must die; all our growth comes to naught if death ends it all."
- C. Where, then, can we find the answer? Philosophy? No, with it we can only speculate.

- D. Jesus alone can answer: •Proved by His
  resurrection (1 Cor 15) •Assured by His promise
  (John 5:28–29)

IV. WHAT IS NEXT, AFTER THE RESURRECTION?

- A. Judgment (Heb 9:27) Our destiny will be
  announced
- B. His appearing and our answering (2 Cor 5:10)

V. WE CAN DETERMINE OUR DESTINY BEFORE DEATH BY SETTING OUR HOUSE IN ORDER

See Isaiah 38:1–21. Our need: hear and obey the Word of God.

A Tribute to Sister Dorcas

Acts 9:36–43

Jack P. Wilhelm

Death is a common experience for all human history, as we are taught in Hebrews 9:27. The Bible speaks of "the death of the wicked" (Prov 11:7, Eccl 8:10), but it also speaks of the death of the righteous as being "precious (Ps 116:15) and further says, "Blessed are the dead who die in the Lord" (Rev 14:13).

Both categories of those deaths are referred to in the book of Acts:

The Wicked	The Righteous
●Judas, Acts 1:15–20	●Stephen, Acts 7:54–60
●Ananias & Sapphira, Acts 5:1–11	●Dorcas, Acts 9:36–43
●Herod, Acts 12:21–24	●James, Acts 12:1-2
	●Eutychus, Acts 20:7-12

Of these 8 who are named, the hope of the righteous stands in stark contrast to the hopelessness of the wicked. This lesson will center on Dorcas and her positive attributes.

I. A BRIEF SKETCH OF DORCAS AS A PERSON

Under the heading of her other name, Tabitha, *Unger's Bible Dictionary* (1066) says she was "... a benevolent Christian widow of Joppa whom Peter restored to life. ... She was probably a

Hellenistic Jewess known to the Greeks by the name Dorcas. ... and to the Hebrews by the Aramaic equivalent. ... The Greeks used Dorcas, i.e. 'female gazelle,' as a term of endearment for their women ..." (Relate other facts about her found in the text.)

II. SOME REASONS WHY DORCAS WAS WORTHY OF TRIBUTE

A. Dorcas was a disciple, v. 36. The word "disciple" means learner and refers to followers of Jesus. Alexander Campbell preferred to use this term in reference to followers of Jesus, though they were later called "Christians" at Antioch (Acts 11:26).

1. John 8:31–32 Continuing in the word makes one a disciple and free.
2. Luke 9:62 One who becomes a disciple must be faithful and not turn back.
3. Matthew 28:18–20 Those who become disciples are expected to lead others to become disciples.
4. Regarding Dorcas, it should be noticed that being a disciple does not make one immune to death. It is a fearful thing to die without having the hope a disciple of Jesus has.

B. Dorcas rendered service by doing what she could while she lived, v. 36 "She was full of good works and charitable deeds which she did."

1. v. 39 "the tunics and garments" were "made while she was with them ..."
2. Many do not want to be active while they can—it is always "what I did in the "good ole days," or 'what I will do when I retire' or 'when I get other things out of the way."
3. Acts 13:36 David "served *his own generation* by the will of God ..."

4. Dorcas rendered unselfish service instead of becoming helpless and making self-centered demands that others serve her.

5. 1 Timothy 5:10 lists several "good works" that Christian women can do. They are especially gifted in showing hospitality and caring for the sick and afflicted.

C. Dorcas was loved and respected by those who knew her best.

1. They went as far as they could go in showing their love: they tenderly prepared her body for burial, they sent for the apostle Peter (v. 38), and they were present and weeping as they remembered all she had done (v. 39).

2. It is commendable that she lived in such a way that those who mourned her passing did not have to pretend to be sad! (Notice the contrast regarding what was said about King Jehoram in 2 Chronicles 21:19–20: "He died in severe pain. And his people made no burning for him, like the burning for his fathers ... and, to no one's sorrow, (he) departed ...")

D. Dorcas exerted a strong, positive influence.

1. Her influence was good *before her death:* She was "full of good works and charitable deeds which she did" (v. 36). Doing "good works" is the way to practice pure religion (Jas 1:27) and to be like Jesus (Acts 10:38). See also 1 Timothy 5:10

2. Her influence was good *after she died:* The survivors were "weeping, showing the tunics and garments which Dorcas had made while she was with them" (v. 39). One's influence always lives longer than he/she

does, but it can be either good or bad. [Notice Mark 14:3–9: "What this woman has done will also be told as a memorial to her." (v.9)]

3. What remembrances will people have *us* after we are gone?

4. Her influence was good *after she was brought back to life:* Peter "presented her alive. ... And it became known throughout all Joppa, and many believed on the Lord" (Acts 9:41–42).

5. We cannot expect immediate miraculous resurrections back to life today. The purpose of miracles was to confirm the Word, which was done (Heb 2:3–4). The same Bible that teaches us that miracles occurred tells us that they ceased (1 Cor 13:8). We are promised a resurrection of the dead, however, when the Lord returns (John 5:28–29; 1 Thess 4:13–18).

6. The good influence of those who have passed on can still be effective in helping us to live right, even as Abel, though dead, still speaks (Heb 11:3–5, 12:1–2).

7. Illustration: The story is told of a college student who thought he had "outgrown" belief in the Bible and resisted obeying the gospel. He gave serious thought to his life, however, when he observed the faith and courage of his Christian mother as she died after a lingering illness. He said to his preacher, "I heard all your sermons and thought I could answer all your "pat" arguments for belief in the Bible. However, I cannot answer the logic and wonderful contentment my mother had as a Christian. I want for myself whatever it was that made my mother what she was." See Psalm 35:14 "I bowed down heavily, as one that mourns for his mother."

8. Timothy was also greatly influenced by the faith that was shown first in his mother and his grandmother (2 Tim 1:5). When the influence of a godly mother is at

its best, it is one of the most powerful forces in the world to convince one of the wisdom of God's plan for the perpetuation of the faith.

Conclusion

Revelation 14:13 affirms a great blessing for those who die in the Lord: "Blessed are the dead who die in the Lord from now on ... that they may rest from their labors, and their works follow them." To die *"in the Lord,"* one must *be in the Lord!* Galatians 3:26–27 and Romans 6:1–5 tell us how to do that.

A Spiritual Readiness Test

2 Timothy 4:6–8

Jack P. Wilhelm

We hear much about tests: • Diagnostic tests e.g. Reading Readiness, etc. • Graduation exams • ACT and SAT tests for college entrance • GRE or other tests for graduate study • Job evaluations or Exit exams.

It is more important for us to think about a spiritual readiness test, so that we may be prepared for eternity.

I. PAUL SAID THAT HE WAS READY.

A. There were several evidences of readiness in different emphases of his life:

1. Romans 1:15 He was *ready to preach the gospel*
2. 2 Corinthians 12:14 He was *ready to go on missions* to preach the gospel, even if his motives were at times questioned by his hearers.
3. Acts 21:13 He was *ready even to die* for what he believed in rather than shirk his duty or deny the Lord.
4. 2 Timothy 4:6–8 He was *ready for an accounting to the Lord* when the end of his earthly life came.

B. See also Philippians 1:12–26. All of the above thoughts were a part of his philosophy.

II. FACTORS THAT CONTRIBUTED TO PAUL'S READINESS

A. Paul severed all earthly loyalties that would keep him from following Christ.

1. He did so *immediately* when he learned the truth (Gal 1:15–16; Acts 9:6, 18, 22:16).
2. He did so *completely* regardless of the cost (Phil 3:7–8, Gal 1:14–16).
3. He did so *continuously* by following through (Acts 9:20, 2 Tim 4:7, Phil 3:13–14).

B. Paul was fruitful in his work, but it was always to the glory of God.

1. 1 Corinthians 3:6–9 "I planted, Apollos watered, but God gave the increase. So then neither he who plants is anything, nor he who waters, but God who gives the increase. Now he who plants and he who waters are one, and each one will receive his own reward according to his own labor. For we are *God's* fellow workers; you are *God's* field, you are *God's* building."
2. 1 Corinthians 3:11 "For no other foundation can anyone lay than that which is laid, which is Jesus Christ."
3. 1 Corinthians 1:10–18 Paul condemned divisiveness caused by unscriptural loyalty to men.

C. Paul was victorious in self-denial.

1. 1 Corinthians 9:22–27 He used the regimen of a rigidly trained athlete to illustrate the way he disciplined himself, lest he should "be disqualified."

2. Galatians 2:20–21 "I have been crucified with Christ;
   it is no longer I who live, but Christ lives in me; and
   the life which I now live in the flesh, I live by faith in
   the Son of God, who loved me and gave Himself for
   me. I do not set aside the grace of God ..."
3. Paul did not say this formula was easy! See Romans
   7:18–19.

D. Paul was faithful in spite of opposition and adversity.

1. 2 Timothy 4:6–8 A fight had to be fought. A faith
   had to be kept. A course had to be finished. He
   approached life's end with strong conviction that he
   had done that.
2. 2 Corinthians 11:23–28 Paul endured many
   problems, and his record of overcoming stood out in
   stark contrast to those of his critics! "Are they
   ministers of Christ?—I speak as a fool—I am more!"
   He gave a list of the many hardships he had endured.
3. Philippians 3:13–14 He pressed on, though his past
   could have held him back: "I do not count myself to
   have apprehended, but one thing I do, forgetting
   those things which are behind and reaching forward
   to those things which are ahead, I press toward the
   goal for the prize of the upward call of God in Christ
   Jesus."
4. His secret? He kept his thinking centered on heavenly
   things: "For our citizenship is in heaven, from which
   we also eagerly wait for the Savior, the Lord Jesus
   Christ, who will transform our lowly body that it may
   be conformed to His glorious body, according to the
   working by which He is able even to subdue all things
   to Himself" (Phil 3:20–21).

Conclusion

Have you ever been fearful as you approached "a final exam"? Perhaps even called on to teach a class (or preach a sermon!) for which you were not prepared? You know the discomfort one feels.

The Bible gives us something to think about as we approach our appearance before God at the Judgment!

- The terrible discomfort of the unprepared can be seen in Matthew 22:11–14, where one at a feast appeared *"with a garment,"* even though such garments were provided and such bold presumption was without excuse!
- There is also the lack of preparation of *the foolish virgins,* as described in Matthew 25:34.

The Bible also gives us a picture of the beautiful blessings and comfort that will be enjoyed by those who are prepared:

- Matthew 20:34: "Come, you blessed of My Father, inherit the kingdom prepared for you from the foundation of the world!"
- Revelation 22:14: "Blessed are those who do His commandments, that they may have the right to the tree of life, and may enter through the gates into the city."
- Revelation 14:13: "Blessed are the dead who die in the Lord from now on. ... they may rest from their labors, and their works follow them." (They will fear no embarrassing disclosures of unforgiven secret things that were a part of their life's history!)
- 1 John 3:19–21: "... We know that we are of the truth, and shall assure our hearts before Him. For if our heart condemns us, God is greater than our heart, and knows all things. Beloved, if our heart does not condemn us, we have confidence toward God."

Is your heart right with God?

WITH THE LORD

JACK P. WILHELM

At the end of a service, a song leader walked up to the pulpit level and began leading the invitation song. His little son, age 3, soon walked up and stood by his side. The reaction of the audience was so noticeable that the minister interrupted at the end of the first stanza and said, "We are all amused at the most natural thing in the world—the desire of a child to be with his father." He then applied it to the concern he felt about wayward Christians in the audience who showed a lack of concern about coming home to be with their heavenly Father." The overriding concern of all of us should be to "be with the Lord." In this lesson, we will explore some progressive relationships that we can experience to "Be With The Lord."

I. THERE IS A SENSE IN WHICH WE ARE NEVER OUT OF THE PRESENCE OF THE LORD.

- A. Psalm 139:1–12 "Where can I go from Your Spirit? Or where can I flee from Your presence?" (v. 7).
- B. Acts 17:27-28 "... He is not far from each one of us; for in Him we live and have our being ..."

- C. Jeremiah 23:24 "Can anyone hide himself in secret places, so I shall not see him? says the Lord. 'Do I not fill heaven and earth?' says the Lord."
- D. The "omnipresence" of God should be a comfort to us, rather than a reason to fear Him.

II. SOME SPECIAL SEQUENCES IN WHICH CHRISTIANS CAN BE WITH THE LORD.

- A. When one obeys the Gospel to become a Christian, he/she begins a new relationship with the Lord.
- 1. Romans 6:3–5 "Therefore we were *buried with Him* through baptism into death, that just as Christ was raised from the dead by the glory of the Father, even so we also should walk in a newness of life ... *we have been united together* in the likeness of His death ..."
- 2. Galatians 3:26–27 "For you are all sons of God through faith in Christ Jesus, for as many of you as were *baptized into Christ* have put on Christ."
- 3. Colossians 3:1–2 One who is *risen with Christ* must seek things above.
- 4. 2 Corinthians 5:17 One who is *in Christ* is a new creature.
- B. When one assembles with Christians for worship, he/she is with the Lord.
- 1. Matthew 18:20 "For where two or three are gathered together in My name, I am *there in the midst of them.*"
- 2. John 20:19, 26 "... when the doors were shut where the disciples were assembled, for fear of the Jews, Jesus came and stood in the midst ... And after eight days, His disciples were again inside, and

Thomas with them. Jesus came, the doors being shut, and stood in the midst, and said, 'Peace to you'!"

- 3. Hebrews 10:25 Christians are commanded not to forsake the assembly. One who can do so casually leaves doubt as to his desire to be with the Lord. It has been said, "If our faith is not strong enough to bring us to worship, is it strong enough to take us to heaven?"

- C. When one renders faithful daily service, he/she is with the Lord.

- 1. 2 John 9 "Whoever transgresses and does not abide in the doctrine of Christ does not have God. He who abides in the doctrine of Christ *has both the Father and the Son.*"

- 2. 1 John 1:7 "If we walk in the light as He is in the light, *we have fellowship with one another,* and the blood of Jesus Christ His Son cleanses us from all sin."

- 3. The Christian who maintains and practices doctrinal purity will be with Christ because the things he will do will involve Christ working through him in his life:

- a. Matthew 18:5 By helping needy children, we are receiving Christ.

- b. Matthew 10:40 When we help God's messengers, it is regarded as an act of receiving Christ.

- c. Colossians 1:27 Paul described what had happened to the Colossians as if it were "Christ in you, the hope of glory."

- D. The faithful Christian can be with Christ when he/she dies.

- 1. Philippians 1:20–24 Paul had a dilemma, whether to abide and help the Christians or to depart and "be with Christ, which is far better." (v.23)

-     2. Revelations 14:13 Great blessings await those "who die in the Lord."
-     3. Ecclesiastes 12:7 After death, "the spirit shall return to God who gave it ..."
-     4. Luke 16:19–31 After death, Lazarus was at rest in the presence of the Lord and His people.
-     5. 1 Thessalonians 4:14 The saved dead ones are with Jesus: "God will bring with Him those who sleep in Jesus."
-     6. Scholars do not agree on just when the timing of this joy will occur, but it is agreed that the faithful can be with the Lord beyond death, so, "Death, where is your sting?" (1 Cor 15:55).
- E. In the ultimate, and most intimate sense, faithful Christians can be with the Lord in their Eternal Home!
-     1. 1 Thessalonians 4:13–18 "Then we who are alive and remain shall be caught up together with them in the clouds to meet the Lord in the air. And thus we shall always be with the Lord. Therefore comfort one another with these words."
-     2. Revelations 21:3 "... and He will dwell with them and they shall be His people. God Himself will be with them and be their God."
-     3. Matthew 25:34 The prepared will be invited to come and enjoy the place prepared for them.
-     4. John 14:1–3 Jesus promised to return and said, "Where I am, there you may be also."
-     5. Even if the how, the what, and the when of our going to be with the Lord are not fully described for us, at least the fact is clearly taught!

Conclusion

If we as Christians have spent our lives here on earth trying to be with the Lord and to approve and do the things He approves, why should we fret and dread God's invitation for us to be with Him in eternity? We will merely be taking the next step in the continuous, progressive relationship of being "with the Lord" that we have already been taking.

Caution: One cannot die "in the Lord" without doing what the Bible teaches us to do to get "into Christ." That procedure is very clearly spelled out for us in Romans 6:3–5 and Galatians 3:26–27.

WORDS OF COMFORT
JACK P. WILHELM

"Blessed are they that mourn for they shall be comforters" (Ray Allen). The need for comfort is universal, and those who have needed it most are capable of giving it best.

I. GOD HAS PROVIDED SPECIAL COMFORT TO HIS PEOPLE IN HIS WORD.

- A. Romans 15:4 "For whatever things were written before were written for our learning, that we through the patience and comfort of the Scriptures might have hope."
- B. 1 Thessalonians 4:18 "Wherefore comfort one another with these words ..."

II. CIRCUMSTANCES WHEN WE NEED COMFORT

- A. We need comfort when in adversity and sickness.
- 1. Job. 6:8, 10 "Oh, that I might have my request ... That I would still have comfort ..."
- 2. Job 10:20 "Are not my days few? Cease! Leave me alone, that I may take a little comfort." Job

was desperate—even regretting that he had been born and wanting to die. As a merchant tests a coin by letting it ring to verify genuineness before putting it in his cash register, God tested the genuineness of Job by his trials.

- B. We need comfort when burdened with discouraging duty.
- 1. Colossians 4:7–11 Paul said that Tychicus, Onesimus, Aristarchus, Mark, and others were fellow workers who had been a comfort to him.
- 2. 1 Thessalonians 5:14 "We exhort you, brethren, warn those who are unruly, comfort the fainthearted, uphold the weak, be patient with all."
- 3. Evangelists and elders need encouragement to avoid "burnout"—though it has been said that you "can't have burnout unless you have first been on fire!"
- C. We need comfort when we have been opposed to doing good.
- 1. 2 Corinthians 7:5–6 "… when we came to Macedonia, our bodies had no rest, but we were troubled on every side. Outside were conflicts; inside were fears. Nevertheless, God, who comforts the downcast, comforted us by the coming of Titus." Notice: Titus gave further comfort by giving a good report about the Corinthians (v. 7). God works with His people. Is He working with us to comfort anyone we know?
- 2. 1 Thessalonians 3:1–3 Paul sent Timothy to encourage others. He was comforted by the report Timothy brought back to him about them, v. 7.
- D. We need comfort when we have decided to make a break from sin and do right.
- 1. 2 Corinthians 2:6–8 (Review the sinful condition described in 1 Corinthians 5 Paul had

urged the Corinthians to correct.) When the offender repented Paul said: "This punishment which was inflicted by the majority is sufficient for such a man, so that, on the contrary, you ought rather to forgive and comfort him, lest perhaps such a one be swallowed up with too much sorrow. Therefore I urge you to reaffirm your love to him."

- 2. A teacher once said, "I work with young people who get in trouble and often get them to begin to turn their lives around. As I urge them to make new, Christian friends, the Christian young people or their parents do not seem to want to accept them, out of fear that bad results might occur. What is the solution to this?" Parents and youth leaders perhaps need to monitor closely and be sure to choose activities and participation levels wisely.

- E. We need comfort in times of sorrow and bereavement.

- 1. Psalm 23:4 "Yea, though I walk through the valley of the shadow of death, I will fear no evil, for thou art with me. Thy rod and thy staff, they comfort me."

- 2. 1 Thessalonians 4:13–18 "Therefore comfort one another with these words." Why were these words of Paul comforting to the Thessalonians?

- a. They were comforting because *of their source*: God had used Paul mightily in trying circumstances, out of which He had delivered him. He could assure them of hope because of his personal experience.

- b. They were words of comfort because *they imparted knowledge and dispelled ignorance*: "I do not want you to be ignorant, brethren, concerning those who have fallen asleep, lest you sorrow as others who have no hope." (v. 13).

- c. They were words of comfort because *they assure us that our departed loved ones have not been annihilated, forgotten, or abandoned:* "God will bring with Him those who sleep in Jesus. ... the dead in Christ will rise first!" (v. 14, 16).
- d. They were words of comfort because *they affirm the return of Christ as He promised, to vindicate our faith in a cynical world:* "For the Lord Himself will descend from heaven, with a shout, with the voice of an archangel, and with the trumpet of God." (v. 16).
- e. They were words of comfort because *they declare a happy, hopeful future for the faithful:* Loved ones in Christ will be reunited and be forever with the Lord, (v. 14–17). "At your right hand are pleasures forevermore" (Psalm 16:11).

Conclusion
Clarence McCartney once said:

"Men fear death as children fear to go in the dark. ... My own experience at many deathbeds has been to the effect that death is its own anesthetist and banishes fear in the minds of the dying. But because so many dread that last experience in life, it will be always true that cowards die many times. The Christian should be the last of all men to fear death." (*McCartney's Illustrations,* 86).

We often say that some act may "haunt a person to his dying day." Perhaps we should warn people more about things that will haunt them "beyond their dying day," as happened to the rich man in Luke 16. See also Matthew 10:28.

The Scriptures offer much comfort to those who "die in the Lord," but little comfort to those who refuse to believe the gospel and obey it (2 Thess 1:7–10).

Comfort is for those who "die in the Lord, ... that they may rest from their labors, and their works follow them" (Rev 14:13).

Funeral Message for Jack Wilhelm
Rickey Collum

I love prayer. It is so amazing that through our mediator, Jesus Christ, we, who are just regular people, can talk to the creator of all things! God answers prayers! I have been asked to pray this afternoon, for the family, for you and for others who are grieving the loss of our brother in Christ.

When someone dies as a faithful Christian, we as fellow Christians know the assurance of Heaven; 1 John 5:12–13 says:

> *He who has the Son has life; he who does not have the Son of God does not have life. These things I have written to you who believe in the name of the Son of God, that you may <u>know</u> that you have eternal life, and that you may continue to believe in the name of the Son of God.*

But even with our knowing Jack's salvation, we selfishly feel the need for him to be with us. You would not believe the people that I have heard just in the last two days, who have said, I would not be an elder if it were not for Jack Wilhelm, I would not be a preacher if it were not for Jack Wilhelm, or I would not be a Christian if it were not for Jack Wilhelm. The weddings, funerals, baptisms, and people who became Christians because of radio or television programs conducted by Jack are more than we can count.

I miss him already. Without Jack Wilhelm, I am just another person sitting in the seat at church, not getting it. Because of him, I am a preacher. He was my mentor and encourager. For the first two years I preached, I would write a sermon and send it to Jack. The first year, he would read it, offer suggestions, and make changes. In the second year, he would mark mistakes and send them back. After two years, he was saying, I believe I am going to use that one next week. He was there when we appointed elders, and there were eleven responses. I didn't know what to do, and he stepped up and said you get half, and I will get the others.

Like you, I love Jack and Mary Alice Wilhelm. If ever two became one, they are your example. While I was helping raise our two boys and not having a father myself to turn to, I would call Jack and Mary Alice; Jack would tell me how it was supposed to be, and Mary Alice would tell me how it really was!

Jack could get you to do things without you knowing he was maneuvering you into doing them. When my boys started to drive, I believe he knew I would struggle to put gas in four cars, so out of the blue, he called and asked me to cut his grass; he was getting too old. The first time I cut that ditch to the side of the house, I fell on the ground exhausted. He came by and said, "It is rough, I had to quit at 75."

To you here today, I know there are a thousand stories just like mine, in this audience. The family would like to thank you for your support and your love.

To the family, I know as much as I loved him, you loved him more, and I want to join with the people here today to ask you to let us help in your sorrow, let us lift you up in prayer, and let us be the phone call when you need to talk. Let us pray!

Also by Cypress Publications

The Christian Life: Chapters for Bible Teachers
by Ed Gallagher

Easing Life's Hurts
by Jack Wilhelm and Bill Bagents

Ecclesiastes: A Document Designed to Disturb
by Coy Roper

Equipping the Saints: A Practical Study of Ephesians 4:11–16
by Bill Bagents and Cory Collins

The Holy Spirit: A Bible Study Guide
by Jack Wilhelm

I AM: A Study of the True and Living God
edited by Jeremy Barrier and Charles R. Webb

Jesus the Christ: Chapters for Bible Teachers
by Ed Gallagher

WHAM! Facing Life's Heavy Hits: Thirteen New Testament Encounters
by Bill Bagents and Laura S. Bagents

WHAM! Facing Life's Heavy Hits: Thirteen Old Testament Encounters
by Bill Bagents and Laura S. Bagents

Wild Transformation
by Matthew Morine

CYPRESS

To see the full catalog of Heritage Christian University Press and its imprint, Cypress Publications, visit www.hcupress.edu